# THE SECRET LETTERS OF A PSYCHOTHERAPIST

Sharlene Sema Raston

# TABLE OF CONTENTS

# Biography

I, Sharlene Raston, author of the book "On the Road to Enlightenment" was born in Harare, Zimbabwe and soon after I moved to Maputo, Mozambique. I studied at the Portuguese school in Maputo, and in 2004 I moved to Pretoria, South Africa. I am a Life Coach and NLP Practitioner, I follow the Cognitive Behavioural Therapy approach on Psychotherapy and Hypnotherapy, Eastern Philosophy and have been registered in Psychometry (PMT 0086835) with the Health Professions Council of South Africa since 2011.

I completed my Honours Degree in Psychology at the University of South Africa (UNISA) and my Bachelor's degree at the University of Pretoria where I specialized in Psychology and Criminology. I completed a Diploma in the various Treatments and Effects of Addictions at the Open College University in the United Kingdom, I did my Life Coach and NLP Certificate through School of Life (South Africa) and own a certificate in Basic principles for First Line Managers from UNISA, SA.

My Psychometric training was carried out through UNISA; I gained a vast amount of knowledge while working in South Africa and got accreditations for the Personal Profile Analysis tool (PPA) at Thomas International, Cognitive Process Profile tool (CPP) at Cognadev and the

Learning Potential Computerised Adapt (LPCAT) developed by Marie De Beer.

I have many years of experience in the corporate world in Management in the Telecommunications Industry and Psychometric Testing. In 2016, I went to London to undergo training in Cognitive Behavioural Hypnotherapy at the UK College of Hypnosis and Hypnotherapy, one of the world's leading accredited hypnotherapy schools specializing in an evidence-based approach. I had also trained in Rational Emotive Behavioural Therapy (REBT) at the CCBT College in London, which is a pioneering form of Cognitive Behavioural Therapy (CBT) developed by Albert Ellis. For my Continuous Learning Development, I had the privilege to attend some seminars from Windy Dryden who is one of the leading practitioners and trainers in the UK in CBT and the first Briton to be accredited in REBT at the Albert Ellis Institute. The fundamental notion about REBT is that it is not the events that happen in our lives that disturb us, but the belief that we hold about the events that disturbs us, in other words, we disturb ourselves.

In 2019, I got certified as a Life Coach and NLP practitioner at School of Life in South Africa.

My work is highly inspired by notorious figures such as the Buddha, Alan Watts, Albert Ellis, Aaron Beck, Windy Dryden, Victor Frankl and many more. As a result, I have combined the knowledge and training I had acquired over the years from the great philosophical thinkers into developing my unique view and perspective.

I will always refer to my present job as play because I wholeheartedly love what I do and at no given moment feel like I am working. I truly love my clients; I see a side of them that is so real, true, raw, and human. In society, everybody is too busy acting like the most influential human being on earth, cold, putting on a mask to chase success — trying to hide their emotions so as not be perceived as weak. It gets to a point that we can no longer know someone for real, due to the mask everyone constantly wears. In the therapy room the mask falls off completely, and I see people's real selves. I manage to see a human being in front of me, and I love it.

My passion for philosophy has been alive from the moment I was exposed to it at the school where I was known as Descartes. Moreover, I am now continuing the chosen path of being a writer.

# Introduction

People who are interested in therapy and want to understand the methods I use to guide my clients into overcoming their several conditions often say things such as: "Okay, so imagine a problem or make up a scenario and then tell me how you will treat the person." This always shocks me and I simply explain that this is not how it works since a session takes an hour and there are many things to explore before coming up with a "cure". Then they say, "Fine, so now imagine someone is having issues in their marriage. What would you advise? And how would you treat them?" – My reply to that, again, is that is not how it works because there is detail surrounding it – and it is so complex as there are theories, structures, methods and tools involved, so it is unrealistic to expect me to provide a cure out of the blue.

Those who know me know that I am solution-oriented, meaning – if by any means I start foreseeing a problem, I automatically play the worst-case scenario in my mind and quickly come up with a solution for it so that I can maintain the desired balance. This works for everything and also in relation to the abovementioned scenario. Therefore, I have decided to develop a guide in the form of letters inspired by the most common real-life issues, struggles or conditions, followed by feedback and suggestions that should allow you to understand how the therapeutic process works, learn exclusive methods and teachings applied in all sorts of areas and benefit from it first-hand.

This can be perceived as an exclusive guide and it might just turn into your best friend.

I hope you enjoy it ☺

# CHAPTER 1
# THE SECRET LETTERS

## Dear Beautiful Soul

First of all, I would like to thank you for contacting me, I really enjoyed our first session. We discussed different issues that we will be dealing with and I will be more than happy to guide you in identifying your goal and give you all the available tools that will definitely help you to achieve your goal as quickly as possible. In order to do that, what I need is your commitment and I am positive we will soon get there.

We have to move in stages. Structure is very important so everything can appear clear for both of us and we know what we are focusing on. I have attached the value & goals spreadsheet that will certainly help you realise where you are at in your life in terms of satisfaction in different areas and where you wish to be.

We have also identified that you tend to feel anxiety (an unhealthy negative emotion), which is the natural response when your mind perceives threat or danger and we discussed that the healthier version of anxiety is concern. Our aim is to move from anxiety to concern. Note that, within CBT, you will find different approaches too — Rational Emotive Behavioural Therapy and Cognitive Therapy — I will be combining the work of the two therapies into our sessions. I have already recommended Mindfulness, which is the practice of being aware of the present moment and connecting with yourself in the present moment. You are more than welcome to do some self-reading on the subject and you will be surprised by the benefits of it.

We spoke about your tendency to do some fortune-telling which leads to worrying, confusion, and blocks you from making decisions as well.

I hope this helps and with the material provided, please try to see how the concepts apply to your own circumstances and how you feel. If you have any questions in the meanwhile, or need any assistance, please feel free to contact me and I will gladly assist you.

# *Dear Beautiful Soul*

Thank you for the feedback, I am glad that you found it helpful. The reason I mentioned boredom or the feeling of losing concentration in my previous communication is because it is perfectly normal and happens to most people – it isn't a sign of not being able to focus, but simply that our minds are always busy with thoughts and we are very accustomed to living in the future or past and are hardly in touch with the present moment.

I like to refer to our mind as a 1-year-old toddler that doesn't listen and is always out and about. It loves to just throw some random thoughts (many of them negative/unhealthy) and when we actually take the thoughts seriously without challenging them, we are more prone to develop emotional disturbance and all those unhealthy negative emotions. Therefore, we need to be able to distinguish SPAM thoughts from logical, rational, helpful and healthy thoughts.

I also suggested that every time a thought goes by during meditation/self-hypnosis, instead of focusing on it, the technique we should use is to become the observer and just observe what is going on and simply watch without any judgements.

You can also imagine yourself sitting in front of a river, putting each thought on a leaf, placing the leaf on the river and watching the current take it away from you. The more we do these exercises, the easier it becomes and the more we focus. The biggest purpose of this is also to discipline/train our minds, which takes time, but with practice we do get there. Being aware of ourselves allows us to stop being a slave to our minds which makes us prone to unhealthy negative emotions.

And by the way, due to the nature of the exercise (relaxation), the idea was for you to feel the way you did, deeply relaxed. So, all good, it seems that we managed to achieve the desired result.

Based on the amount of effort you are putting and your willingness to overcome these emotions, you will definitely recover sooner than you expect.

# Dear Beautiful Soul

It was nice seeing you today and I am happy to see that you look great and balanced in many ways. There are indeed certain situations that trigger negative emotions in you, however, they are normal reactions from a human being when faced with adversities.

We spoke about the ABCDE model, which I strongly suggest you start working on. You can choose two situations of which you experienced an unpleasant emotion and you can work on using the model.

By observing your goals exercise, I see that you tend to imagine the worst-case scenario quite often and react to that; you experience this in your relationship mostly. This could be seen as a tendency to do some fortune-telling which leads to worrying, confusion and may block you from making decisions as well.

Note that if you wish to work with an issue of which you tend to catastrophize, we can do an exercise together called De-catastrophizing — this is very good for anxiety-related issues and we will actually challenge the fears that are causing you to feel anxious.

We might need to also work on assertiveness — to find ways for you to express yourself and be able to get your message across comfortably. This will allow us to tackle the small issues you tend to face with people on a regular basis where you feel that they are crossing your boundaries.

We haven't tackled the career path aspect that you find extremely important and you seem dissatisfied, however, I see that you tend to get overwhelmed by anxiety in many areas of your life and it has been affecting you negatively. I think this should be a priority for us to actively work on it, uncover what is underneath it and find ways to cope with it.

In the meantime, I would recommend that you do some relaxation exercises that I believe will be of benefit to you. They are just 14 minutes long and will help you to relax and remove any tension in your body.

# Dear Beautiful Soul

Attached is the wheel of life that I explained to you during the session which will help you have an overall understanding of where you are in life right now and where you would like to be. Setting goals is a fundamental step in giving us direction to take.

We spoke about assertiveness and I am going to share with you in a nutshell what we discussed, but don't put any pressure on taking action at this stage, as we have to work on your priorities and stages. In other words, it is important that we identify what your priorities are, the goals, and the emotions and start making progress accordingly.

Four-Steps of Assertiveness:

1. Describe the plain facts of the situation. (These are the plain facts...)

2. Acknowledge the other person's viewpoint. (I understand your position is this...)

3. Assert your own viewpoint. (This is how I feel about things... I feel pretty angry about... I have a right...)

4. Propose a resolution. (This is what I want to happen... I am going to... I want you to...)

Assertion is extremely important to adopt in our everyday life — and the best example I can give is how we train dogs to behave the way we want them to. We train them through rewards and punishments, with consistency and, eventually, the behaviour is changed and it becomes automatic. In other words, we need to also incorporate that in our daily lives.

With regards to the conditions I spoke about, you can research a bit regarding "narcissists", and in the process, you will find interesting concepts such as "Gaslighting" which you may or may not relate to.

If you have any further questions, please feel free to reach out and I will gladly assist you.

# Dear Beautiful Soul

First of all, I would like to thank you for contacting me. I really enjoyed our first session. We discussed different issues which were:

1. The fact that you have changed a lot from when you started your relationship up to today and you wish to get back to the old you, where you engage in different activities and find enjoyment in certain things in life. We came to the conclusion that you haven't been engaging in many of the activities you used to find enjoyment in, and therefore, it is natural that you will feel less happy.

2. The break up could definitely be related to the loss of drive in things. Note that you have been living a certain kind of life for the past couple of years, in a certain environment. Therefore, there is a chance that there will be some adaptation in your new routine — which might bring some sort of initial discomfort, but as you go along, your mind and body may get used to it. So far, you are not going through the "expected" grieving process, but there's nothing wrong with that.

"Never pretend to a love of which you do not feel, as love is not ours to command." Alan Watts

I think that quote may apply to any emotion you are experiencing, or lack of it. There's no need to feel guilty about it — remember to just be.

3. Loss of motivation and procrastination — we spoke about doing things if we want to see change. You know it in theory and it's time to put it into practice. However, we tend to want fast results, instant gratification, which is human nature and how things have been set up lately that make us become less patient. It is important that we maintain the behaviour, and as an example, try to think about the process of fitness. When you start going to the gym, it takes time to see great results and it also depends fully on the effort you put in. If you stop after a week, you will see no results, but if you continue, after a month you will see significant results. In the same way, if you see the results after a month and you stop exercising, you will go back to where you started. The process of change takes a similar route and involves the same dedication. After you have been to the gym for a while, you will also notice that you keep on improving by the day and you get more and more results which keeps you motivated. So, try to keep that example in mind and apply it to every change you wish to make in your daily life.

We spoke about procrastination and to try out the 5-minute rule — to sit down and commit yourself for 5 minutes only — and see what happens.

And with regards to getting things done, just ask yourself — what is stopping you from doing it? Motivation? Not everything in life is exciting and requires motivation, many times we've got to just get up and do things whether they are fun or not, and trust me, if you start getting things done, you might just have a sense of achievement at the end of the day which is far more rewarding than no achievement. Again, don't force yourself to do anything — but instead, think about the end result of actually doing it and what it may feel like to have accomplished things.

We have to move in stages, and structure is very important so everything can appear clear for both of us and we know what we are focusing on.

I hope this helps. If you have any questions in the meantime or need any assistance, please feel free to contact me and I will gladly assist you.

# Dear Beautiful Soul

In the last session, we talked about the various issues you have in terms of behaviours and emotions. Especially with regard to your ex-partner who has a tendency to get nervous easily since she doesn't take the time to listen to other people.

What I have observed is that each of you are constantly defensive and listen to respond. Your brain is equivalent to a full cup of tea, and when the other one speaks, it is similar to trying to put more tea in a cup that is full, as a result, the tea simply spills. The only way either of you can assimilate what is said is by listening and showing empathy by lowering the ball. For a variety of reasons and also because it is you doing therapy— we have come to the conclusion that this behaviour and attitude should come from you and you will see the advantages of incorporating it into your communication.

When you communicate, it is important that you do not focus on the details of what she is talking about or on concrete examples — because she speaks broadly about a set of things rather than one thing.

We did the ABCDE exercise:

**A (Event)**

In a conversation, she said things that from your perspective are not entirely true. E.g.: You didn't try to reconcile... You didn't respect her condition...

**B (Beliefs)**

1. She is lying

2. Why is she thinking like this and not like me?

**C (Consequence — Emotions and Behaviours)**

Angry, frustrated

Verbally aggressive, speak louder

Nervous

Tremble and unable to express yourself

Hot-headed and unable to focus on anything more serenely

**D (Dispute) — Dispute Convictions**

1. Is there evidence that she is lying intentionally?

2. Is it logical to think this way?

3. Is it beneficial to think this way?

**E (Establishing new beliefs)**

1. Why is she thinking like that? What's behind everything she says?

2. From my perspective, things did not happen as she describes it. Why does she feel the way she does?

3. Maybe I should pay more attention to what she says in order to sympathize and understand her perspective

because only then will she feel heard. She will probably calm down and things will likely get better.

We discussed about assertiveness, and below you can find the steps to the assertive process:

Describe the facts about the situation:

1. Make a summary in an objective and impersonal way, focusing only on the relevant facts. Do not use emotions, assumptions or any kind of interpretation.

E.g. "Based on my observation, I detected the following factors..."

2. Recognize the person's point of view: Reflect politely about the other person's point of view in terms of thoughts and feelings so he/she feels understood — and does not feel the need to reiterate your opinion on the subject.

E.g. "I realize that your position is...", "I realize that from your point of view..."

3. Show assertiveness in your point of view: Summarize your objections and feelings in a concise and clear manner. Be congruent, speak in the first person to make sure they understand clearly what you want to convey.

E.g. "I feel... about the situation...

"I feel quite... about...

"I have the right to..."

4. Suggest a solution: State what attitude you will take and what your expectation about her behaviour is. Suggest an agreement between the two parties or a solution, and state that the first step should be taken immediately if possible.

E.g. "I wish it would happen..."

"What am I going to do from now on is..."

You can take a look, analyse and give me feedback on the next step. I would advise you to use the techniques — put them into practice, and after that, we will arrange a session to evaluate how it went and how to improve communication and the situation.

# Dear Beautiful Soul

These are the Emotion Skills we spoke about in order to decrease anger, fear, shame and sadness.

After practicing mindfulness I suggest we focus on the interpersonal skills that will certainly have a great impact into your communication skills with your loved ones. The dialectical behavioural therapy (DBT) acronym is **GIVE**:

Gentle: Approach the other party in a delicate non-threatening manner, avoiding attacks and judgemental statements.

(Act) Interested: By genuinely listening to the other party without interrupting.

Validate: Acknowledge the other person's viewpoint.

Easy Manner: Assume a light-hearted and humorous tone.

The **STOP** technique when you find yourself feeling angry or overwhelmed with emotions:

Stop

Take a deep breath and a step back

Observe the situation

Proceed effectively

Another effective technique is called **DEAR MAN**:

**D** – Describe: Describe the situation in objectively and without judgment.
**E** – Express your feelings to the other party, how you interpret the situation and therefore how it makes you feel.
**A** – Assert: Be assertive about your wishes, i.e. clearly state what you do or do not want.
**R** – Reinforce why the desired outcome is desirable, and reward people who respond positively to the request.
**M** – Mindful: Be mindful and present in the moment, focused on the current goal. You might just conclude that the two of you share the same goal – happiness and understanding.
**A** – Appear: Appear confident, adopting a confident posture and tone, and maintain eye contact.
**N** – Negotiate: Be willing to negotiate and give in order to get, with the understanding that both parties have valid needs and feelings

So, the homework would be for you to try these techniques throughout the week at least twice, and then you can write down:

1: What happened?

2: How you felt afterwards.

# Dear Beautiful Soul

So, today, we discussed everything that you have been involved with work-wise, which shows that you are a very dynamic person and you enjoy getting involved in different things and are also good at what you do. However, as you stated, you are only one person and by focusing on certain things, you end up slacking on others — which is okay (when it is a conscious decision) but it seems that you are, to an extent, going with the flow. The disadvantage of this is that you do not have a clear idea of where exactly you are going as everything seems to be all over the place.

We came to the conclusion that, at this stage, you do not have a clearly defined goal, you know you want to travel and be comfortable financially, maintain the lifestyle you have always had and, in fact, have a bit more financial freedom, but that is not a clearly defined goal and does not assist you in a concrete manner. Therefore, I have mentioned that when you set a goal, it is important for you to make sure that the goal is SMART.

**SMART** stands for:

Specific — clear, simple, concrete and you can explain it in a specific language.

Measurable — you will know when you have to achieve it.

Achievable — it is within your sphere of control; consistent with your other goals and "ecologically sound".

Relevant — is it relevant to the problems you are facing? Consistent with your fundamental values? A higher priority than other goals at this time?

Time-limited — do you know when you will achieve your goal? What would be an achievable deadline? Is it broken down enough? Is it short-term enough?

So, once you've set up your goal, you can look at the factors above and improve on them until you feel that it is as SMART as possible. From then, you can easily start working on your options, and plan a proper schedule that will get you as close as possible to achieving the goal.

You will be able to identify what is a priority for you and what isn't and you will know where you are heading. You will find that it will be a lot more gratifying than just going with the flow.

Ask yourself:

1. What would you advise someone you care about to do in a similar situation?

2. What would a creative person do?

3. What would a wise person do?

4. What would a courageous person do?

5. What would be the easiest thing to do?

6. What would be the most effective solution possible?

7. Overall, what do you think the best or most realistic solution would be?

So...what will be your first step?

Brainstorm as many alternative solutions as possible and list them:

Solution 1

Pros

(Short-term)

(Long-term)

Cons

(Short-term)

(Long-term)

Solution 2

....

Solution 3

.....

What obstacles do you encounter? How can you deal with them?

When are you going to put your plan into practice?

What can stop you from putting it into practice?


How will you make sure you will definitely do this?


Based on the nature of the problem, I found this method to be the most appropriate and it should help you break down the information and get a clear view of what you want, to weigh up the alternatives and remember — as much as this exercise may appear exhausting — this is a personal investment and you are taking time for yourself and on your own personal development. Each question has its relevance as it makes you think it through from different angles. Once you have explored thoroughly and things are clear and organized in your mind, it will be much easier to move on to the next step — the plan of action and implementing it.

What can stop you from putting it into practice? This is a very important question. Us human beings tend to procrastinate and just do what is more comfortable and easy, so you need to be aware of the factors that may interfere with that and know what strategy you will use to not allow it to take the best of you.

I hope this helps and please reach out if you have any further questions. If there's anything else you want me to add or clarify, let me know and please feel free to share your results and I will gladly provide you with feedback too.

And at the first stage, I would advise you to share your goal with me once you set it so I can have a look and give you some insight on trying to make it as SMART as possible before proceeding.

Please let me know if you think this exercise will be helpful. And anything else you may feel you want me to tackle at this stage.

# Dear Beautiful Soul

It was such a pleasure meeting you today. You gave me an overall view of the situation in general and where you are emotionally and rationally too. I believe that your current situation is completely normal and there is some degree of expectation that you would go through such a period, as life is not normally smooth and nothing is permanent. Especially our feelings that can be compared at times with the wind, it is in constant change and never just stays smooth.

My only advice as a therapist would be that whatever decision you make, you need to think it through and look at all the aspects and make sure that you don't overlook aspects that in future you may find to be of relevance. There is absolutely no rush for you to make any decision and remember that the part of your brain that gets activated when you are "in love" or "infatuated" or being moved by "passion" is the exact same part that gets activated when you are high on drugs, and as you know, someone that is being moved by a "drug" does not think clearly.

It is very important that you get in touch fully with your rational side too because that is your helper — long-term.

I also mentioned that whatever decision you make, I believe you will be fine. Us as humans always are, as long as it is well thought out and done in the healthiest manner.

I recommended you do a cost-benefit analysis, which means to actually look at all the alternatives you have and outweigh the pros and cons. If you do this, you might see your ideas more clearly and really be more aware of what it could look like to choose other alternatives. Of course, the data for every situation is infinite but we can work with what we know and can predict somehow.

So, basically, what I am asking you to do is really look into every single aspect in-depth, you can take as much time as you want.

Contact me at any time if you need any clarity or even to give me feedback and tell me that you do not find the exercise relevant and we can work on making it more relevant and tackle certain aspects that you may find more helpful. Remember that the best investment you can make is in your own personal development — there is no right or wrong, there are simply paths.

# Dear Beautiful Soul

I hope you found our session helpful and it gave you more insight on how your thoughts/beliefs may have been contributing to the intensity of the feelings of anxiety you have been experiencing.

We did the ABC model together and I will share with you a YouTube video that explains how you do it. As homework, I suggest that you work with one unhealthy negative emotion you may experience and change it to the healthier negative emotion version. In our next session, I can also give you a quick insight into the different unhealthy negative emotions and their healthier versions.

Now, let's look at the exercise we did:

**Activating Event: (trigger)** — it is very important to be aware of the trigger because, as soon as it comes, it is what you tell yourself that determines how much it will escalate.

Chest Sensation

Lack of Breath

**Belief:** What did you tell yourself?

- I am never going to get rid of this

- This is not normal

- Something MUST be wrong. (Notice the "Must" — which is a reflection of a rigid and inflexible belief that automatically leads to unhealthy negative emotions...)

Notice: Were you finding this sensation unbearable? The end of the world? Extremely awful? — This shows low frustration tolerance. So, there is a need to bring awareness from that and move to High Frustration Tolerance. It is crap, it is bad — but you can bear it, you can cope and it is not the end of the world — you can tell yourself that.

**Consequences (feelings, emotions, behaviour):** What did the unhealthy belief lead you to experience?

Tense, sad, overwhelmed, tired, crying, aggravating headaches

**Alternative Belief**: What would be a more helpful way of looking at the "event"?

- There you go, this bloody anxiety again, it is not comfortable, I do not enjoy it, it is unpleasant BUT it is not the end of the world, I can bear it and cope with it.

- These sensations are normal to experience as they are simply signs of anxiety. They are pretty uncomfortable but they are normal symptoms of it and I shall just focus on my coping mechanisms, then, in no time, I will feel better, from past experience and through scientific evidence — anxiety can reach its higher levels but it does not last – eventually, it drops.

- Thinking that I shall be entitled not to feel it may be unrealistic — most of us tend to experience some anxiety at some point in our lives but I will cope and it's okay. I have been coping my entire life by the way, otherwise, I wouldn't be standing here.

Remember to also give yourself some credit — you have been doing a good job so far and you have already used some coping mechanisms that have worked. It is important to be aware and continue to make use of them. Like any activity, it takes practice and with it – we will get there. The secret is to continue using whichever mechanism we find successful.

Above, I used my own words and you shall obviously use your own words and how you identify yourself better. In our next sessions, we will implement these ideas, we will work on the negative thoughts — move to the healthier version in the situations during hypnotherapy and we will see how changing your thinking will change your bodily sensations and emotions. It will be interesting and you shall be able to take the new feelings into your everyday life.

# Dear Beautiful Soul

You mentioned that your goal is "to become a better person" so it can manifest in your behaviour towards others, most importantly, your family. You would like to improve on your self-image, worry less, and portray a better image in relation to others and yourself. You have identified the "anger issues" as being the top priority for us to work with and it is very important that you can develop the skills to manage it in a healthier manner.

Note that "being a better person" or "being a better father or husband" continue to be fully vague abstract concepts — when we set a goal, it is of high importance that we make sure the goal is SMART (Specific, Measurable, Achievable, Realistic and Time-Bound) — and therefore, being specific is extremely important as it will allow us to measure your improvement and the success of the therapy session. If we make the goal specific, it will be much easier for us to identify when you achieve it.

In this specific scenario, I feel that we should agree that one of the goals is to move from anger (an unhealthy negative emotion) to annoyance (a healthy negative emotion) — I will elaborate on this in person.

I have explained to you that, in CBT, we do Psychoeducation as the first step and it is equally important that, after this, we move to the behavioural aspect of it and start putting the teachings into practice gradually. In other words, it is of high importance that you start incorporating everything you learn into your daily life, and inevitably, you will start seeing the positive changes. I did mention that you have been having this behaviour pattern and a set of rigid beliefs for too many years, which means that your brain is used to thinking in a certain way and, therefore, to respond to it accordingly — which means that it may take some time for you to incorporate the new set of skills, but the amount of time is highly dependent on the amount of dedication you put into it, your willingness and how flexible you are in this process.

I am more than happy to work together and will do my best to provide you with the guidance that will allow us to achieve your goal.

Please keep in mind that we believe that what is causing all of this is the B — your belief system and not the A — the events, and you can do as much yoga as you want, engage in as much reiki as you wish, do as much meditation as you wish — but if you don't change the B, you shall continue to fall in the same C pattern — unhealthy negative emotions and behaviour. We will work on this on a deeper level, so no worries, one step at a time. But you will find that it is way simpler than you imagined it to be.

Below, you can find some links that will give you an overall understanding of CBT/REBT (note that Rational Emotive Behavioural Therapy is one of the ramifications of Cognitive Behavioural Therapy), which is the perspective that we will be using the most during our sessions and, of course, I will borrow methods from other forms of therapy within CBT and possibly Dialectical Behavioural Therapy considering that it is related to "anger issues".

# Dear Beautiful Soul

As a follow-up with regards to our meeting today, I wanted to ask you to complete the PHQ-9 (Patient Health Questionnaire-9) which objectifies and assesses the degree of depression severity via questionnaire. It takes about 1 minute to complete. This is just so we can assess your depression levels at this stage. So, please fill it out and send me the link once you have filled it in so I can take a look.

I would like to also ask you for some feedback with regards to the therapy up to today. Have you been finding it helpful and do you see any improvements in your emotions and your day-to-day life? If yes, which type of improvements have you noticed?

If no, could you please advise me on what you would want to focus more on and also some improvements from my side too to make the therapy sessions more fruitful?

Change does not happen overnight as it requires wisdom and practice. The practical side of it, which is the behavioural change, is crucial for change. Theory alone will not take you any further unless it is applied.

It is much easier to stay in our comfort zone but the disadvantage is that we don't see much improvement and it leads to frustration as you have been feeling for a while. Note that the first steps may be uncomfortable, but as you practice, it shall become natural. I am making reference to this as I am referring mostly to the "assertiveness".

I am tackling this because the events you have described of being referred to in an offensive tone is completely unacceptable. And please think of yourself as your best friend, someone that you adore, care for and stand up for and think about the importance of being more assertive in a way that people know their boundaries so you can protect yourself from any type of verbal abuse or offensive remark. There could be an underlying issue that may have contributed to the lack of assertiveness which could be related to self-esteem. You are a wonderful, beautiful, intelligent, kind and sweet person, it is clear that you are good at what you do and don't allow anyone to tell you otherwise.

I fully encourage you to use the assertiveness skills we have discussed so it gives you a sense of control and strength. It is highly important to make sure that you are not taken advantage of due to your kindness. Make sure that you get what you have paid for and promised.

You spoke about the guilt you experience by playing around on the internet — note that you are only playing around on the internet because that is what you feel like doing. If you wanted to do something else, you would be doing something else as you have equal resources too. It is okay to do nothing and there is nothing wrong with that — you can use your time in whichever way you prefer. However, if you are keen to work on your goal, it looks like you are procrastinating as you are postponing something that is in your best interest. That's fine, we all procrastinate pretty often, so there's no need to feel guilty as it appears to be part of our nature. I suggest that you try to use the 5-minute rule and promise yourself that you will work on your projects for 5 minutes every day. After 5 minutes, you are free to stop or to continue if you wish. But the rule is 5 minutes a day. It is a step and each step shall get you closer to your goal. On the other hand, no actions = no results.

Remember that those negative emotions you are experiencing such as guilt — you are creating them yourself through the negative perspective you are using to interpret "playing around". You can play around as much as you want, there is nothing wrong with that — without making yourself feel guilty about it.

As Alan Watts says, the meaning of life is simply to be alive and enjoy the dance, and yet everyone is rushing around with great panic as if there is something very important to achieve. Human beings suffer because they take too seriously what the gods made for fun.

# Dear Beautiful Soul

Thanks for coming today, I truly enjoyed our session and hope you are getting more clarity and thinking in healthier ways to tackle the problem you are faced with.

At first, we discussed behavioural factors, that if changed, you would probably tolerate your situation in a positive manner.

You mentioned that you don't really tackle many issues in order to avoid confrontation, and we discussed assertiveness in order to get your message across in the most effective way.

You tend to feel guilt and anxiety — completely normal — we haven't tackled the emotions yet and I hope we will still work on those emotions as they are unhealthy negative emotions.

I asked you to formulate the problem so we know what we are working with, and you stated that:

You no longer want to be married and you wish to get a divorce in the most peaceful manner.

I asked you what had stopped you from achieving your goal, and you mentioned: the pressure you feel from your spouse and your family.

The most feared outcome is a big argument as a result of taking action.

The most undesired outcome is, you do not want to be misinterpreted by your loved ones.

Some undesired outcomes, possible pressure from your loved ones and society to stay in the marriage.

What resources do you have: Some direct family members that fully understand where you are coming from, they want the best for you and are willing to provide you with the support you definitely need at this stage.

How can we minimize the "feared outcome" and the undesired outcome?

We have agreed that the best plan of action would be to be very strong about your convictions and decision and communicate the message in a diligent manner to ensure full understanding and empathy.

I would fully recommend that you write down everything — use the four steps of assertiveness when you do so.

Lastly, once the above steps have been completed successfully, it will be time to take the most difficult and feared step: Action.

Note: the nature, complexity and seriousness of the steps you will soon take require diligent communication, strength, objectiveness and focus. Your speech shall also sound mature and well thought out too.

I am now going to share with you a speech from Alan Watts in relation to marriage:

"As for marriage, there is nothing wrong with it except the legal institution. The natural event of a man and woman living in constant companionship, with or without children, is an admirable arrangement which works to the degree one does not insist that it must work, and does not treat one's partner as property. Another being regarded as property is automatically a doll.

Whenever I perform a ceremony of marriage for personal friends, I give some such discourse as this:

'What I am about to say may at first sound depressing and even cynical, but I think you will not find it so in practice. There are three things I would have you bear in mind. The first is that as you now behold one another, you are probably seeing each other at your best. All things disintegrate in time, and as the years go by you will tend to get worse rather than better.

Do not, therefore, go into marriage with projects for improving each other. Growth may happen, but it cannot be forced.

The second has to do with emotional honesty. Never pretend to a love which you do not actually feel, for love is not ours to command. For the same reason, do not require love from your partner as a duty, for love given in this spirit doesn't ring true, and gives no pleasure to the other.

The third is that you do not so cling to one another as to commit mutual strangulation. You are not each other's chattels, and you must so trust your partner as to allow full freedom to be the being that he and she is. If you observe these things your marriage will have surer ground than can be afforded by any formal contract or promise, however solemn and legally binding.' A couple that would object to this discourse should not marry." — Alan Watts

I believe that if you go through the material provided today, time and focus, you will have a more clear idea about the situation and solutions provided. This will assist you not only in your decision making but also to be more aware of the possible short-term and long-term advantages and disadvantages. As you can see — all that was needed was structure and asking the "right", productive or "relevant" questions.

Enjoy the rest of your weekend — and if you don't conclude, we can always work together on our next session as this is relevant. And the reason why it's relevant is because it is a decision that will change the course of your life significantly.

Make sure to keep in mind — the best improvement you can make is in your own personal development.

# Dear Beautiful Soul

During the session, we agreed that from now on you will do the following:

1. You will identify a gym, preferably with a personal trainer or a gym that has classes of interest to you: It can be Zumba, yoga, spinning... You have absolutely nothing to lose by experimenting.

2. You'll include in your weekly calendar a day to take care of the following:

a) Skin — it may be with clay that you do quite well... or the method you find most suitable for you.

You can put on light makeup that usually gives a positive touch and makes you feel more beautiful.

b) You'll think of some way to take care of your hair — something as simple as curling your hair makes a big difference. You can identify a hairstylist who can help you with ideas on how to take care of and perhaps innovate your hair in some way.

c) You will always be sure that you have painted your nails and are always beautiful — so that you look at your nails and like what you see.

d) You will look at your wardrobe and see different ways you can innovate the way you look and feel. Simple things like necklaces and earrings — notorious things always make a difference — so that whenever you look in the mirror — you really like what you see... this will automatically be reflected in the way your husband sees you. Pay much more attention to yourself and you will start to feel that you are more independent — this will naturally arouse interest and curiosity.

Nowadays, with unlimited information on Google, you can simply search: " how to do a makeover " or " makeover ideas " or something along those lines that can give you some ideas.

So, your homework is what you see above, and in our session, I will be very happy to see that you have already made your calendar and that you have started to practice the homework — I promise that we will see very positive results. I think that you have already noticed the strategy I choose to use is the opposite strategy of what you have been doing, and instead of focusing on making him change, let's use the reverse strategy — let's change your behaviour. One more suggestion: From now on, you promise that when he gets home, even if he's late, you will welcome him with a smile and be in a good mood — this will also arouse curiosity in him to understand what is going on.

# Dear Beautiful Soul

It was a pleasure having the session with you today and seeing the great progress you have made since our first session. Like you mentioned, I am dealing with two completely different people.

The former you had many doubts about your goals in life and yourself to the point that you didn't think you were a good worker because you made mistakes periodically and could not handle the responsibilities of your promotion. Clearly, this perspective was not shared by the people of the company as you did it and you were chosen for a position of greater responsibility.

You said that you often felt like giving up. Today, you are performing the position that you were terrified of and that filled your head with "what ifs..." constantly and it is going well. I mention this example so that whenever you are afraid of leaving your comfort zone and following your dreams or goals, remember the movie you made about this situation, how unnecessary it was and if you had listened to the movie, you would not be where you are today. In fact, you would be where you always were and frustrated.

Your growth/achievements happened pretty fast and I think one of the biggest factors that led to this was the fact that you really dedicated yourself, focused on knowledge and learning more and more unfailingly and had results.

Today, you mentioned having the desire to travel to other continents and invest in your business idea. But then you said that what would really affect you negatively would be to see that you are still stuck and that you are not moving on the business side.

The choice you make should be based on:

1. What do you value most: Traveling or your professional independence?

2. How much do you need monetarily for each of these ideas? Write down the expenses of each thing in detail, including the visa, accommodation, how much internal travel (e.g. Asia) you need, food, extra money, etc.

3. In terms of business, it would be important to calculate the return as well — so you will know how much you will earn each month.

4. Write your salary on paper and your fixed and variable monthly expenses (you can also include what you normally spend to be with friends and such), and see how much is left.

5. Calculate the remaining amount you will always have each month and have an idea of how much money you can collect by a certain date.

6. Open an extra bank account so that whenever you enter your salary, you can immediately transfer the money to that account and not touch the money. From

that moment on, you will begin to turn to the value you delineated as if the other money did not exist.

7. After allocating a date and knowing how much you will have by that date, which of the goals could you achieve or how many? Always remember your priorities and what's most important to you: short-term and long-term.

8. It's important that you have this all organized, preferably in the neatest Excel format. I will repeat again that you will have to sacrifice certain things in order to allocate time to achieve your goals. I would advise you to pick 3 days a week to focus on just that – and I believe that as you see results, you are more willing to work and will always be proud of every accomplishment. The most important part of a business is the business plan — so you already have the guide, and I also saw that you have a to-do list, so you can allocate dates for everything on the list... so every time you sit down, you know exactly what you have to do.

And lastly, I also said that it is important to align your short and long-term visions and objectives and to define your business; the target audience, the marketing strategy, the company presentation, prices, how long it will take to deliver each order, who you will work with and so on. We talked about Google Docs — which you could implement in your department (to explore better) — we talked about Fiverr — the site/application where you will find several freelancers for different purposes at very affordable prices, watch out for unreliable sellers.

I look forward to your feedback. Have a great week!

# Dear Beautiful Soul

I hope you enjoyed our session today. I am pleased to hear that you have been experiencing some positive results already — it makes me really happy and fulfilled. I can definitely see great improvements in comparison to the space you were at during our first session. You appeared to be confused, your ideas were all over the place, and you were giving importance and spending a considerable amount of time worrying about things that do not deserve such dedication/attention. And you now sound a lot more balanced, calm, and your ideas are getting more and clearer. You have been a fantastic client — as you are committed and working with me towards achieving your goal. Well done! You even set time aside to do your Business Plan already — you are definitely going at a fantastic pace.

Today, we mainly spoke about habits that you wish to adjust and the overwhelming feelings you experience when you hear the word "break-up".

For the impulsive habits, we agreed that you will plan and do it consciously let's say three times a week as you wish at whatever times you find ideal. This way, you will fulfil your needs already and, therefore, it may reduce the probability of having to do it impulsively. With time we can decrease the exposure. If you don't manage to stick to it straight away, there is nothing wrong with that. All you need to do is continue trying/practicing — you shall get there (just like driving).

With regards to your habits — if you find yourself feeling negative or low from it, simply stop. You can stop as there is nothing forcing you to do it. So, saying that you can't stop is not realistic nor true. You may say that you enjoy it too much, which makes you struggle to stop doing it, but that is obviously another story. I encourage you to stop simply to show yourself that you are in control and you can — as opposed to being a slave of your mind and habits. Remember that, whether you tell yourself that you can or that you can't, it is true.

Lastly, we discussed the impact the word "break-up" has on you. I suggested you do what we call Cognitive Diffusion, of which — one of the techniques is to repeat the word plenty of times — like a hundred times — and don't worry if you are bored, just continue doing it with different sounds and rhythms and so forth until the word becomes meaningless.

This exercise is highly important because it helps you to get to a point of which words become just words... meaningless... so you can easily perceive it as SPAM and not invoke any emotions — please do it and I shall look forward to the feedback in our following session.

# Dear Beautiful Soul

I trust you are well, this is just a quick note regarding our last session and the homework we discussed.

I do suspect that your fear of separating is the factor that overwhelms you the most, and that fear seems to be so strong that you appear to be able to endure any situation, as destructive as it may be, in order to ensure that it shall not happen. Unfortunately, if this is the case, this fear is preventing you from having task-relevant behaviours as your brain is leading you to perceive it as being a nasty person.

There is a huge difference between assertiveness and being nasty... and between standing up for your values, setting boundaries, being aware of your rights as an individual and being nasty.

When asked the question what do you want from a partner? You first told me aspects that a robot could fulfil easily — but when asked for a deeper answer which includes characteristics and expectations of what you wish to have, you went blank and you appeared to not be able to come up with at least one quality. This is extremely worrying as it is a reflection of complete lack of self-awareness and self-neglect. It could also be one of the reasons why you tend to not defend your rights or yourself from any kind of emotional or verbal abuse — as you completely dismiss your emotional needs. I am not asking you to be able to answer: Who am I? As that would be an unrealistic request, but to be in touch with yourself.

Every single time you show confusion or anything related to the path you're both going to take — you try to play out the different scenarios the other person could come up with, measure the probabilities and so forth and, therefore, you put your partner in a position to be the one and only decision-maker and you shall be the follower.

I would ask you to please:

(1) Sit down for a while, without any rush or interruption, close your eyes and let the last couple of months' episodes play in your mind, and watch it as the third person as if you are watching a movie — not from your perspective. Observe all the characters, including you — how each of them behave and how each of them responds to it... and then you may sit down and write the story. A story in which you describe the main characters, behaviours, events and so forth — and their emotions too. Please bring this story with you to our next session.

On a different note, simply:

(2) Ask yourself, what do I want? What do I expect from a partner?

(3) What are my values in relation to relationships?

Please put some thought into it — and try to go through it and check if what you feel is closer to love, attachment or an addiction.

I hope this helps and have a lovely day further.

# Dear Beautiful Soul

I am very happy to hear that you are already seeing improvements in your relationship and the communication between the two of you — which is very important. I would suggest that you don't worry too much about chasing feelings or wanting a certain type of feeling from his side — but on the practicality of things instead. And I believe that, as the harmony sets in more and more, and you restore your friendship — everything will naturally fall into place.

I would also highlight the fact that our memories in relation to the past are very much distorted — even though sometimes we may not think so. But that blur you mentioned many people experience because even though we may think that we remember something accurately, studies have proven that our memory is not trustworthy. Keeping this in mind — I am not entirely sure to what extent it would be helpful to review each and every single incident, but as we discussed, I think the two of you may both just need acknowledgement from each other, empathy and recognition for everything you have been through. As it was certainly not easy for either of you. And therefore, I would certainly support this discussion.

Let me know how it goes and I hope you enjoy the book — I am certain that it will assist you very much in understanding our unhealthy emotions and behaviour — and how to move to the healthier version.

# Dear Beautiful Soul

I hope you are okay after our session and finding closure and acceptance of the loss — as it is not easy for anyone. Surely, he should be going through his mourning period, which is an important period that needs to be gone through unfortunately.

Well, what we need to do now is an evaluation of our therapy sessions too — we have spoken and discussed many things and ideas but it continues to be a drag for you to implement any — and I see no drive in you either in terms of making the effort to change things or being more proactive to make changes — which leads to serious procrastination as well as keeping you stuck in the same position.

And if this means that therapy alone is not sufficient, I highly recommend that we combine it with a psychiatrist and we can talk about what has worked and what hasn't worked and why.

Maybe I can make a report to one and we could work together to get things going — normally it works much better than therapy alone if both professionals and you as a client put the effort in and make things happen.

I don't want this year to be a drag from last year in any of our lives — we need to see progress, identify what is not allowing the progress, get the necessary medical help together with the counselling skills — which doesn't only involve opening up and having someone to listen to and share ideas with, but also get stuff going.

But we need to work on removing this anchor that is keeping you stuck.

Please think about this email and let me know if we can commit to this. You have two weeks to start evaluating the real things you need changed in your life and fully — what is stopping you. We can go through it intensively too.

Please promise to yourself that this will not be another depressing year. You have too much going for you. It is time to stop allowing invisible obstacles to get in your way and stop you from succeeding.

# Dear lovely Couple,

It was such a pleasure seeing you guys today and I am glad to see that there have already been some great improvements in this short period of time.

I totally understand why the homework was not done yet and I hope you have understood the importance of the exercise we did today with the role play. This helps to decrease the probability of procrastination as we are all aware that it is not easy at all to take steps that have never been taken before. As you can see, discussing it through in detail, putting it on paper and going through all the steps makes it more real, easier to do and less abstract.

Charles, remember what Anne said — even if you manage to get 30% through, it would be more than enough for her. What is most important is for her to feel that you have her back and you stand up for her. As she is alone here, she would like to feel and perceive you as her rock.

Anne, remember to also be aware and appreciate all the efforts Charles has been trying to make all along to keep the family together, his appreciation for you and desire to have you in his life as his wife. He has definitely met many people throughout his life and has chosen you as his partner and the one he wants to spend his life with — in harmony. His lack of communication with his family is not a reflection of lack of care at all, but simply because it is 100% outside of his comfort zone to do so. Men are so difficult, to hear a man saying he wants to marry you and spend the rest of his life with you is not common at all — trust me. What I see most is men panicking when women bring out these ideas — look around.

So, I hope that you can see the value and rareness in his behaviour which means that you are extremely precious. To seek therapy — through my experience — it's mostly the women and to get the men to agree is always a battle and takes time. These are pure stats and behaviours that have been observed. There is also a great deal of investment, not only financially and with time — of which Charles has been willing to do because he is fighting for what he values dearly. Remember this and also show your appreciation. I saw the way you looked at him today and how you felt — it was very obvious to see your eyes shining.

Unfortunately, being in our comfort zone all the time does not have great results and, at times, we have to step out of it, go through the effort for the benefit of our own relationship, wellbeing and growth too. There is a huge difference between aggressive speaking and assertiveness. And for as long as we are not assertive, our families will continue to treat us as kids and how they think they should treat us, setting boundaries is of extreme importance in all areas of our lives.

As I mentioned — I would strongly advise that this is perceived as a serious commitment and that it will be done regardless. For your own benefit and in order for things to go forward, I would guess that your family would also appreciate a chat as it will help them understand the distancing. And the purpose of the chat is to bring the harmony back, remove as much resentment as possible as well as minimize any probability of future uncomfortable situations — things are not immediate but I am sure that they will gradually get there.

We discussed that it was important to give an overview of your spouse background and this is to show that she is not being a brat at all — it has simply been new to her.

I am positive that the conversation will be much easier than you imagine. It will flow, there will be interaction and remember to always defend Anne's point of view now that you understand it clearly and will be able to portray it in the most pacific way.

I hope you guys have fun tomorrow, having drinks out and just let go of the baggage and live in the here and now. Make it an evening like in the old times, as we all still have the "young and free soul" within us. Work on getting back to being friends, and I am sure you can't go wrong. If one of you start an argument — how about eventually you look at each other, smile and laugh — and just see how you are just being unnecessarily upset — laugh about it. Then discuss the fact that there's no need to argue. Normally, if one laughs, it increases the probability of the other one laughing.

# Dear Beautiful Soul

You asked for any advice I could suggest on how to deal with you to get the best results in the working environment. You do appear to be very cautious, detailed in your approach to things and motivated by security. I believe that it is very important that your boss gives you the freedom to refer back to him/her at any time as it will bring a sense of reassurance and security during the decision-making processes (mostly in areas that you are not very familiar with). I would equally suggest for any task that is given to you — which he/she provides as much detail as possible as to what is expected from you — this goes hand in hand with the fact that you are cautious in the decision-making process and you are driven by security too.

Note that for the Personal Profile Analysis (PPA), we also have reports that have been designed for that specific purpose. It is called: "How to manage 'X'…"– usually, both parties take the test and that way we get a full understanding of how to maximize the performance, motivators, what not to do, and so forth.

Based on the premise that you are in a leadership position, I would suggest that you also take some time to reflect and assess your influential skills. Which include developing more interpersonal relationships within the organization, assertiveness, and communication skills that will undoubtedly lead people to feel the warmth within the organization and bring a sense of family; these skills also allow you to be more influential towards your team as they incorporate leadership skills. In addition to that, the "sense of family" within the organization leads to great results and also contributes to a sense of motivation within the team although it is important that there are boundaries too as we need to ensure that we are going towards a professionally high performing team.

Note that PPA tests are to evaluate our behaviour in the work environment, not personal, and therefore, it does make sense that most of the staff show similarities in their profiles.

Another observation I made is that the staff do not tend to speak up, share their opinions and appear to have a great fear of making mistakes too. The desire to not make mistakes is fantastic and needed, however, it could be more rewarding if the desire would lead to concern as opposed to fear. Fear is one of the characteristics of anxiety, and therefore, an unhealthy negative emotion — which leads to task-irrelevant behaviours such as check and recheck the work continuously and it directly affects the speed of work.

On the same note, I have identified that the "fear" they experience is due to the rigidity and low tolerance to mistakes. This fear they experience appears to also be interconnected with the "sense of trust ".

Some employees did show discontentment with the zero tolerance for mistakes as, unfortunately, as humans, one of our main characteristics is imperfection. However, in the current situation, it came to my knowledge that if by any chance a mistake does happen, there is a probability of some sort of punishment or negative consequences which appear to be more rigid as opposed to constructive — so it reinforces the fear in them. Note that usually if someone is more concerned about not making a mistake, it directly affects the quality of the work as the preoccupation influences the amount of focus on performing the task as well as the speed.

I believe the weekend away retreat at the beach resort was good and insightful as a first stage, as it allowed me to understand greatly the nature of your work, your profiles and the challenges you have been facing.

Note that we did not place enough focus on goals for the company, conflict resolution, problem resolution (in terms of identifying the problems, the causes of it, brainstorming solutions to solve the problems, the obstacles that may be encountered to solve the problems, the most effective solutions, and the implementation plan).

It is equally important to develop a plan of action with clearly defined steps. The abovementioned topics are of great importance, and therefore, I strongly recommend that in a couple of months, we have a follow-up retreat of which we strongly tackle the current issues you are all facing, work on them in detail and to also place greater focus on building a stronger, motivated team.

I have compiled a follow-up program of which I would be happy to share with you so we can discuss this in greater detail.

Have a lovely day further.

# Dear Beautiful Soul

It was good seeing you today and I am very happy to hear that you've been finding value in our therapy sessions.

I have not explained in detail the model of emotional disturbance — although I have mentioned that one of the main reasons are the demands that we usually put on ourselves, others, or the world. In other words, all the "shoulds", "musts" and "have tos'.

Also, thoughts such as, "everything must happen the way I want it to, when I want it to". And we believe that thoughts are the primary thing which affects our emotions and our behaviour — it is all interconnected. Therefore, it is ideal to replace the demands with preferences. That way, we may still experience a negative emotion, but it will be a healthy negative emotion as opposed to an unhealthy negative emotion. An example of a healthy negative emotion is "sadness" and its counterpart is "depression". The aim is not to eliminate negative emotions but to experience them in a healthy manner instead, which is more realistic, logical, rational and helpful. Another example could be experiencing concern as opposed to anxiety.

Other triggers are: Low frustration tolerance and the aim would be to develop higher frustration tolerance. And we can spot this when we find ourselves saying: "I cannot bear being in traffic... It is the end of the world." — This can be replaced with preferences too: "I do not enjoy being in traffic but it is not the end of the world".

Awfulising: In CBT, the term refers to 100% bad — when we perceive a situation as literally the end of the world when, in fact, we are catastrophizing. Because it is not that bad.

Self-damming — we do this by rating ourselves or someone else based on one event. For example: Perceiving oneself as a failure (making it absolute) for failing an exam or not achieving the target for the month — ignoring all the achievements and qualities someone has.

By this, you may conclude that the reality is — we disturb ourselves with our own irrational view on things. This exercise takes practice but once you are aware of it, it becomes much easier to make the switch to healthier alternative beliefs instead.

As a homework assignment for the week, complete a self-reflection exercise of which you use a recent and vivid example of a situation that you experienced unhealthy negative emotions, and therefore, behaved accordingly, and when you look back you recognize that you may have exaggerated in some way and you could have approached it in a healthier manner.

Please do the exercise and bring it to our next session as it will allow me to evaluate and provide you with constructive feedback.

## Self-Reflection

Choose a problem to work on, one that was either triggered during our sessions or a current life problem that you experienced unhealthy negative emotions.

1.  After reflecting on the problem / an event in your life, how did you feel?  (Use your own terminology in expressing your feelings, e.g. upset, unhappy, cross, nervous etc)

2. What triggered your feelings? Describe what happened. (A – Activating event).

3. What thoughts were you having when you experienced the feeling/s described in your answer to Q1? (Cognitive Consequences)

4.  What did you feel like doing when you experienced the feeling/s you have described in your answer to Q1? (Action Tendency)

5. What did you do when you experienced the feeling/s you described in your answer to Q1? (Behaviour)

Identify your feelings (healthy or unhealthy); you should use terms like anxious, concerned, disappointment, hurt etc.

6.  Of the emotions you have identified, which was the dominant or most intense unhealthy negative feeling you experienced, or which one do you want to work on first?

7.   At that moment (when you experienced the most intense unhealthy negative emotion), in order for you not to have felt the unhealthy negative emotion; in an ideal world, what was your most cherished desire or wish?

A) For example, 'my most cherished desire was for everyone to think 'I am smart'.

B) Write down your most cherished desire or wish in the form of demands (musts, shoulds, ought to's, have to's etc.) For example, 'everyone must think I am smart'.

You have now identified your unhealthy MUST belief.

8.   How bad did you feel when you were experiencing the emotion identified? E.g. 'It was absolutely awful', or, 'It was bad but not awful'.

9.   How difficult did it feel when you were experiencing the emotion? E.g. 'It was unbearable. 'or 'it was difficult for me but I could handle it'.

10. How did you rate yourself/someone else/the world, because of it? (Self / other/ world damming). E.g. 'I accepted myself', or, 'I am useless/bad/worthless/failure'.

11. What have you learnt from your reflection?

12. How could you think differently about the event you have described, in a way which would be more constructive and helpful for you? (Construct a healthy alternative belief – one that is flexible, consistent with reality and which helps you move toward your wants/desires/goals).

13. What could you do differently, that would be more helpful and constructive for you?

(Think about the importance of acting against your tendencies and in accordance with the healthy belief you have constructed on Q12)

14. How can you reinforce what you have learnt?

# Dear Beautiful Soul

Awareness of our thoughts, feelings and behaviour and how it all connects is the key, so try to understand what thoughts really go through your mind — just sit down and take some time to write everything that comes to your mind — without making a judgement or manipulating your thoughts. Through that, we can have a better understanding of what is going on in your mind, what could be contributing to how you feel, and consequently, the current situation.

Make an appointment at a Spa, do your nails, go to the salon and do whatever you wish that would bring a sense of new and make you feel even more beautiful than you already are. Dress up, start doing sports/gym/activity/yoga — whatever you enjoy doing...

I have come to the definite conclusion that men are chasers and they like to chase and seduce. If you are doing all the work for him, you leave him with no space to do it. So, try to no longer chase him and give him reasons for him to chase you himself. Make yourself noticeable for him and I promise that, naturally, things will start changing in the opposite direction. Remember, this is not playing games as it will be good for you in many ways.

# Dear Beautiful Soul

As you may have read on my website, I do follow the Cognitive Behavioural approach, specifically Rational Emotive Behavioural therapy and the same approach for hypnotherapy too, which is evidence-based. In other words, it is not the common type we usually see on stage, nor do you go into a trance. I facilitate the process by allowing you to get into a deep relaxation state, 100% aware, and you follow my suggestions by using your imagination.

Although CBT is goal-focused, we haven't yet discussed what expectations you have from the therapy sessions and the main problems you wish to address.

The events you went through recently are indeed deep and it is expected that you would feel hurt and go through the "grieving" process. I do not think that it is ideal to skip the process and to not feel sad because that is the natural response. And when you do let yourself experience it, you might just get bored and naturally move on. The reality is that the more we avoid something, the more it intensifies. The more you tell your brain "don't", you are making a command to your brain to do the exact thing that you are trying to avoid. For example: "Try not to think about a pink elephant" - what did your brain just do? Yes, it thought about the pink elephant! Why? Because the brain doesn't know what "don't" means!

So, remember that our brains are like machines — and you program them, don't you? The whole idea would be to train the brain into the desired outcome you want.

So, the most important question is, what do you want?

Once you know, let me know — I will do my best to help you achieve it.

Note that the purpose of having therapy ranges from wanting to overcome an emotion, wanting changes in certain areas, resolving conflicts all the way, to having therapy out of choice. As an example, I have some clients that have been seeing me weekly for years already. They find it helpful to take an hour a week and simply discuss their week, emotions, events and so forth, in a safe environment, and hear an objective perception of things.

You appear to have great qualities, you have done great work with people and with your previous partner too, which you are fully aware of, and you are a living example that the past does not determine who you are nor what your future will look like; it does contribute to an extent but not fully. It is a choice and you have chosen to succeed and be a wonderful person, so tap your shoulder for that.

You have made a point regarding your choice of man — if you do want a different outcome from what you have been getting, it's important that you change your approach — this will allow you to get a different result. This is something that shall be important to explore too and the reasons behind it.

And you are correct, it is not your job to fix everyone — imagine how difficult it is to fix yourself, so what is the probability that you could fix everyone else? In my case, it is my job to "fix" people but this is out of their free will and desire to change — so much so that they invest in it. You will never find me trying to "fix" people outside of work because, in that scenario, it is not my job. Of course, when approached and asked for insight, I am more than happy to assist. And one of the hardest lessons that I also had to learn is that we cannot fix everyone.

I agree with what you said: they sense that you are a loving, giving person and probably an empath and they get closer. People that usually suck your energy are called energy vampires.

"Empaths tend to typically enter relationships thinking they can help the other person, and they often end up giving all of their energy to the other person."

Awareness of our thoughts, feelings and behaviour and how it all connects is the key — so try to understand what thoughts really go through your mind. Just sit down and take some time to write everything that comes to your mind — without making any judgement or manipulating the thoughts. That way, we can have a better understanding of what is going on in your mind, what could be contributing to how you feel, and consequently, the current situation. A good time to do this could also be when you cannot sleep or when you wake up too early and your mind starts to race.

Note that the work we shall be doing together is a process and it is important that you reflect on the homework and identify which ways you can relate to the material — ways that you could be disturbing yourself due to your beliefs and thoughts.

# Dear Beautiful Soul

As we went through the values exercise, you were able to notice whether or not you live in alignment with those values, and if not, you have 2 choices — to drop the value and replace it with a different one, or change your behaviours and begin living in alignment with your values.

I would recommend that you spend a bit more time contemplating on your values exercise and identify your top priority values. That way, it will allow you to set goals that align with at least your top three values. Could it be that by spending more time focusing on what you value the most it could increase the probability of living an inspiring, meaningful and more fulfilling life?

You spoke about the fact that you value and enjoy using your imagination — that is a great thing as everything starts from our imagination, and once our mind imagines it — it makes it a lot easier to live by and achieve.

From what I remember (you may check to confirm the facts), Walt Disney did have two chairs, one was the imagination chair and the other the "how to execute" chair. And by sitting in his imagination chair, that's when he imagined Disney Land, and they started working on it. Apparently, he died a couple of years before the project was concluded and, in the opening, someone said:

"I wish Walt was here to see what this looks like." and someone else stepped in and said: "Walt knows exactly what this looks like because he was the one that imagined this".

Our minds are super powerful and even though we use a very small percentage of our conscious mind, our subconscious mind does not have limits, which includes our imagination, and by doing that, we can then pass the information to our conscious mind and go a lot bigger.

As we spoke about in the therapy session, the 24 hours we have per day will not change, and therefore, it is important that we do things based on our higher values :)

With regards to using the tools, if we think in terms of: "The story I am telling myself...", "The way I perceive is..." on its own, it not only leads us to be aware that it is not a fact but our interpretation, but it also gives room for the other person to discuss, share their motives and reasons, or what really happened. You are very lucky that you have a partner that is very open for improvement, even though you focus on it more as you choose greatness over average, he does cooperate — this is a really great quality, and as you wondered: "Why don't others focus on that?" This is because they don't see the importance of having a strong foundation.

It could also be that it is not part of their value system and they are not aware of it.

Imagination is so powerful and you use it so diligently that when we decided to play with the hypothesis of simply — "stop making effort", you quickly imagined it, managed to feel what it would be like and you did not enjoy the feeling, so you knew that it was not the answer. For someone else, it could be the scenario of trying to test it for a week and see what happens — you didn't have to go through the entire process as you were able to diligently imagine the feeling.

What stands out to me the most — which I have come to the conclusion that it was highly responsible for many problems within my relationships, whether romantic or otherwise — is the concept of distortion: Our attempt to make sense of this world, we will attribute meanings to events based on our existing maps. "Cognitive bias that distorts our view from the world" — The map is NOT the territory. We love to assume things. And this applies even in the therapy session, hence the importance of me repeating my understanding to confirm if it is correct. My lecturer once said, if you think you know the answer, ask 10 more questions.

In your case, you might identify with the concept of "Illusion of Control" — Which is our belief that we can control or influence outcomes, even when we can't. This is probably why you feel more confident at work, as you have a large degree of influence on the outcome. When it comes to other areas, it can become a bit tricky (just like for people that are super health-conscious, it does not mean that they cannot fall ill), and as I said, the idea would not be to stop working on things to achieve greatness but to simply accept that, many times, regardless of the effort we put in, it will not directly determine the outcome.

# Dear Beautiful Soul

I am happy that you decided to work on your anger issues, note that it is very admirable and you will find that it will make a huge difference to your life and relationships once we manage to work on your perception of things, and therefore, minimize the impulsive behaviour.

Note that the example you gave me regarding your friends — it is understandable and expected that you would feel the way you did because the reality is that they crossed the line with you. And therefore, I do not think we should work on completely removing the emotion "anger" as that is a natural reaction of a human being. Also, there are no wrong feelings — they just take off on their own. So, there's nothing wrong with that — but what is important is how we respond to the situation and ensure that we experience healthy anger — I will explain the difference during our next meeting.

There were three points we mentioned that I have asked you to put into practice as from today — and when I see you next week, I will ask you to give me 2 examples you applied it to and the outcome of it:

1- Empathy, put yourself in the other person's shoes and make sure you understand where they are coming from and why they think or behaved the way they did. Acknowledge that you understand where they are coming from by repeating what they say in different words and say things such as: "If I was in your position,

I would also think that..." After that, you can say your point of view. Note that the communication is not to prove any of the parties to be right but to understand each other, and if you find the need, make suggestions.

2- Interpretation/Distortion — make sure that you are not making a judgement based on the story you are telling yourself but to make sure that you understand the story instead by asking. In other words, do not take your hypothesis as a fact. Do not make assumptions.

3- Be Aware of the Trigger — what triggered you from the moment you were calm to when you were angry? There is always a trigger — so please be aware of yourself to allow you to identify and let me know in our following session.

4- Generalizations – For example, "The people in the restaurant were laughing at the girl because the girl is Asian and the English do not like immigrants" — where did you get this conclusion from? Do ALL people in England dislike Asians? Even the Queen? Where is the evidence for that? Remember, that is the story you are telling yourself but there is no evidence to back it up.

5- Confirmation Bias — When you hold a set of beliefs such as: "The people in the restaurant were laughing at the girl because the girl is Asian and English do not like Asians" and your brain looks for evidence and therefore interprets an event as a confirmation of your belief.

Our brains are machines and we choose how to program them, make sure you make choices that will benefit you and help you live a happier life instead.

# Dear Beautiful Soul

In this specific scenario, it seems that your most important goal is to reduce your feelings of anxiety so you can have a pleasant trip to New Zeland. That sounds fair, although to use hypnosis to get you on the plane does have great benefits, I believe that it is more ideal to tackle the issues that lead to the anxiety you tend to experience.

In my case, I have been hypnotised many times and managed to tackle unhealthy thoughts that led to unhelpful emotions and behaviour. I had a HUGE fear of the aeroplane but love travelling at the same time. I would also experience anxiety the evening before and it was highly unpleasant. As we know — being exhausted and the entire entertainment on the plane definitely helps as it's very difficult to feel anxious for too long. Regardless, I did use hypnosis to make it go away and it's fully gone now and, strangely enough, I learnt to enjoy it a lot more as opposed to feeling anxious. My son also contributed to this, as when I travelled with him, he was so excited about the entire experience — and that was very eye-opening as it was living proof that it is NOT the event (being on the plane) that caused the feelings of anxiety, but rather my PERCEPTION of it that caused it. I was literally causing all my negative emotions myself.

Today, enjoy the take-off, enjoy looking down, the clouds, looking at the sky, being able to switch off for some hours and being in a setting that I don't have to do anything. As you can see, the reasons for my phobia were more related to safety though; an extreme fear of death and perceiving turbulence as a threat — so learning that turbulences mean nothing more than changes in wind speed as opposed to "something wrong" also played a huge role. As my brain stopped associating that with a threat: Classical Conditioning. So, besides the work I did, which also included identifying the triggers, the replace the unhealthy thoughts that would cross my mind that led to anxiety, the added thoughts I had as an interpretation of anxiety which led to increased anxiety (meta-emotions — feeling anxious due to feeling anxious — the emotion doubles), together with the awareness of the high levels of safety in aviation certainly played a role. In addition to that, I had to tackle my fear of death too — which was seriously intense — and this aspect, Alan Watts is fully responsible for reducing greatly and helped me to rather accept it as a process of nature. Fear of Flying, I used Cognitive Behavioural Therapy & Hypnotherapy. Fear of Death, I spent a significant amount of time learning the teachings from Alan Watts, Buddhist masters, religion knowledge and Sadhguru.

I did explain to you the model of emotional disturbance, as I have told you that you are disturbing yourself with the set of beliefs you have regarding many aspects of life. And when I mention beliefs, I refer to:

- Demands — shoulds and musts as opposed to preferences

- **Awfulizing** — rating a situation as 100% bad. "If I enter the aeroplane and I get a panic attack, **it will be the end of**

**the world"**; the healthier version is: "I do not enjoy being on the aeroplane for such a long period of time nor the probability of having a panic attack there. But if it does happen, it will definitely not be the end of the world. I will cope and I have shown great capacity to cope in the past, it is unpleasant but I am very lucky that anxiety or panic attacks ARE NOT DANGEROUS in any way. If my heart starts racing, if I feel that tight thing in my chest, it will go away with time. In fact, all I need to do is not feed it, not pay too much attention to it, take deep breaths for a while and distract myself — soon enough, it will go away."

- **Low frustration tolerance** and to move to high frustration tolerance. "I cannot bear the fact that I might have a panic attack on the aeroplane" — The healthier counterpart: "It's unpleasant but I know I can bear it, it is really not the end of the world".

- **Self-damming** — Rating oneself based on one experience or incident. "My speech was not outstanding during my presentation, and therefore, I am a failure." Healthier version: "I did not make the best speech during my presentation, I would have loved to have done a better job, but it's okay, I will learn from the mistakes I made in order to do a better job in the next one. Besides, I am a human being, and therefore, prone to making mistakes and worthy of unconditional love. I CANNOT get away from making mistakes, I will make a lot more in the future and it is absolutely necessary that it happens as it will give me the opportunity to grow and become wiser."

Have you ever seen a motivational speaker, a successful person that did not fail many times? We hear about them all the time. Even the Harry Potter book was rejected by various publishing companies — and look now.

Many people love to call me lucky because I have my own practice and am doing pretty well with little to no marketing, but I have new clients every week who come through recommendations from existing clients — constantly. They say I am lucky to have written a book...they forget the entire struggle I went through, the amount of sacrifices I had to make over the years, the amount of studying, which also included going to London and being away from my son for almost a year. They have no idea that I had this dream for my entire life, and I approached plenty of places where my application was rejected, I applied for countless jobs — all rejected. It took me LITERALLY 12 years to get to where I am today and finally live my dream. But I was not ready to give up, even though I was faced with countless rejections, I wasn't ready to give up. On the same note, I also left my job and started from scratch — so there was no luck there at all. The only thing was that I knew what I wanted and was willing to pay the price for it. Hence the importance of being able to answer the question:

What do I want?

Imagine if I gave up everything because of all the failures and rejections?

I want to highlight that homework recommendations are of extreme importance in order to make the process smooth, more effective and so results can be seen faster too.

CBT is very, very powerful if you learn it and start applying it – life-changing. In addition to that, Alan Watts was the main philosopher that contributed to the strength I have developed over the years, I will explain this more in person.

In my book 'On the Road to Enlightenment', I covered all these concepts in a very easy to read and valuable way, and on a regular basis, I get messages from people thanking me as when they feel anxious — those words calm them down and most people tend to relate to my journey. Last night, I also got a message from someone saying that it was her travel companion too. If you want a holistic explanation of everything — I definitely recommend it.

You spoke about feeling vulnerable — I would strongly suggest that you don't waste your emotions or thoughts on this specific thing. This is my job and I really love it and respect all of you that are strong enough to open up, discuss your battles with the ultimate goal of self-development.

The one you were and are speaking to now is not "Sharlene" but "The Ultimate Therapist" — two different roles and behaviours and I am happy that I have managed to master that too and be able to separate both things.

# *Dear Beautiful Soul*

There is something called purpose, passion, something that gives us drive to live, to feel happy and it is literally available for all of us. I find that plenty of people are constantly keeping busy with the conscious aim of not having to sit with themselves.

 What are they running away from?

 What's so bad about sitting with your thoughts?

Remember — we are not our thoughts. On the same note, it is important to not give too much credibility to every single thought that pops in our minds. The more credibility you give to irrational thoughts, the more stressed you get which influences directly on your behaviour.

There are countless methods of meditation, the one that resonates with me is — watching my thoughts, my feelings without being in a hurry, without trying to control them — but simply watch.

 By doing this I learn to make the separation between myself and the observer self.

One of the main causes of emotional disturbances are indeed due to unhealthy thoughts of which we give credibility to and perceive them as the ultimate truth.

When we learn to be present and listen to our thoughts this allows us to effectively identify SPAM (unhealthy negative thoughts that sabotage us), minimize them and replace them with constructive thoughts. Once you identify the SPAM, you are free to choose on whether you would like to feed it or not.

We live with ourselves, and therefore it is ideal that we learn about ourselves and what we are passionate about. But, a vast majority of people are not able to answer the simple question:

"What would you do if money were no object?"

If you cannot answer that question, it is equivalent as asking someone for directions and the person asks:

- Where are you going?

And you reply:

- I am not sure!

- Well, if that is the case any road will take you there.

# Dear Beautiful Soul

Is it worth following your heart?

I have taken some time to observe the amount of people that I have met and are passionate about what they do for living. Sadly, very few. People are usually motivated by the stability of an income, the fear of the unknown, some form of status they feel it's important for them to maintain or have and totally dismiss their natural skills, their passion, their dreams and funny enough they put it to the side and say: "I will attend to that later" – as if they have all the time in the world to do so and rather leave it for the lovely future that never arrives.

Our work takes a large and significant part of our lives, we spend more time at work than in any other activity and I wonder why many people are so depressed!

A handful of people come to me on a regular basis and ask me for guidance in following their passion but are not ready to pay the price of leaving their comfort zone and go into the unknown. They want an easy and fast way around it, together with the feeling of security and a guarantee that there will be no failure in the process. Well, that mind set is the main blockage they have. Why? Because one of the main characteristics of an entrepreneur is the capacity to take calculated risks and to be aware that there will be failure in the process. I am not saying maybe, I am saying that it will happen. This is not about, "I will do my best not to fail and panic about it" but to be aware that failure is inevitable and shall be embraced simply because it is the most important ingredient for growth, learning and success.

On the other hand, if you really love what you do, you will naturally place great focus on it, become an expert and consequently get a good fee for it.

Is there a market for my skills? Anything you are interested in doing you will also find people interested in it too, so no need to worry too much.

I am not going to deceive you, taking risks is certainly difficult, scary and may feel dangerous but in my view, it is not as scary as getting to the end of our lives and ask ourselves:

-    What if I have done it?

# Dear Beautiful Soul

It seems that your most important goal is to reduce your feelings of anxiety, to diminish your feelings of pain and the unhealthy recurrent thoughts that are interfering with your mental and emotional wellbeing! The importance of tackling these emotions is mainly because it is interfering with other activities such as when you did not enjoy your safari due to the fear of having a panic attack. In addition to that, you also mentioned that the anxiety or frustration is, unfortunately, having a negative effect on your mood, which can then affect your relationship with those around you.

In our next session, I will focus on teaching you things, sharing ideas, and will start sharing tools too — you will find it very helpful and you will see how easy it is to use your brain wisely to your own advantage as opposed to sabotaging yourself.

Note that I am also a licensed coach, and therefore, if you would like some coaching for developing goals, awareness of your values and priorities — you shall find that you will be living a more meaningful and fulfilling life.

You are a very beautiful, intelligent, well-spoken, unique, adventurous individual — and I promise that you have no reason to ever feel that you are not good enough. YOU ARE! Besides, good enough for what? Who's good enough? What scale are you using to measure this?

One of the most valuable things I have learnt in the past years is that, as an individual, I am unique and great. It is not fair on me to compare myself with anyone else because we are different people with different passions, values, experiences and goals. If by any means I start imitating other mental health practitioners — I am going to lose my essence and authenticity as a person and therapist. My experience in life, my values and approaches to things makes me unique and special. And this goes for you as well. I found that self-love is so important!

You have also mentioned the desire to assess if you are in the ideal path at the moment – career-wise, so we can look into that too! I am extremely passionate about uncovering the passion in others — this is because from the moment I decided to follow what I love, I did not work 1 more day in my life! Because I love what I do! And when that happens — success comes naturally, there is no chasing anything at all. The days become lighter, more fulfilling, interesting and I no longer hate Mondays ever since I left the corporate world and decided to go to London, specialize, and take off on my own. Therefore, I would love to explore that with you too.

# Dear Beautiful Soul

I explained the Wheel of Life exercise to you. On the internet, they have a tool that you can use to score each area of your life and it will automatically draw it for you and give you a good picture of where you feel you are at the moment in all areas, you can then download the PDF and keep it aside.

After that, I would suggest that you spend some time with your imagination and just imagine without limits the woman you envision yourself to be. You may spend some time daydreaming about that, and once you feel ready, you can write down on each sticky note the words that come to your mind, regardless of what they are. One or two words per sticky note is sufficient.

Once you are happy. You can organize the words into three piles — sort them out in the criteria that you think should be sorted. After that, you can organize the piles in order of importance from left to right. Then, sort the individual sticky notes in each pile according to importance from top to bottom. And you may have a look and contemplate on your dreams — probably things that you already know, although this method will help you gain clarity as you will move to setting your goals.

Lastly, you can move to the Values and Goals exercise of which you explore what would being fulfilled in each area look like to you. Remember what I mentioned — if it is not an area that you value as much, you don't need to spend much time there. Just focus on the areas that you truly value as it will undoubtedly contribute for you to enjoy a more meaningful and fulfilled life. What conditions do you believe would be ideal to be present in that will allow you to feel more fulfilled in the areas that you value?

Note, these exercises do not have a right or wrong answer, just follow your instinct and what you think will be valuable for you – meaning, you can also adapt as you go along as the main purpose is your experience and clarity.

I do hope that you enjoy it. I am definitely looking forward to see you, hear your feedback and move to the next steps.

I love these processes of self-discovery and being in touch with ourselves, it is a beautiful process and it brings such great feelings. The one thing that we don't lack are tools to assist us in the process.

NB: I did explain to you that the best way to be able to get rid of unhealthy negative beliefs is through disputation questions. You have now learnt how to identify the unhealthy negative belief that leads to the unhealthy negative emotion: Anxiety. The healthy negative emotion would be: Concern — as having concern allows you to have task-relevant behaviours as opposed to anxiety that leads you to blockages and affects performance.

Please find attached the disputing questions that you may use to remove your unhealthy beliefs. Usually, there are not many unhealthy beliefs, and once you manage to identify, dispute and establish new beliefs, most things start to fall into place, and soon your brain will also do it automatically — due to practice.

# Dear Beautiful Soul

I was thinking about the conversation we had, and in order to have an idea about the treatment plan, I thought it was important to share some knowledge in the area of psychology which I believe will be beneficial to share.

1. Recent scientific studies prove that the use of marijuana, unfortunately, has a huge potential to cause schizophrenia, especially if one has tendencies. Cannabis itself already causes these symptoms of paranoia, voices and psychotic symptoms. So, when consumed by someone with a tendency to develop psychosis, it easily leads to schizophrenia. A very interesting factor in psychology is that it is very difficult to understand precisely what leads to the return of psychoses. Usually, they are assumptions and a combination of factors.

However, in the case of schizophrenia, they claim that cannabis really assumes great responsibility. If you stop early, you can reverse the scenario. Another factor that came to my mind is the tendency that people have to defend marijuana a lot. But what happens is that cannabis oil has proven to do well for many conditions, but without THC (the component that makes a person get high) and what is usually sold to smoke, has exaggerated doses of THC. However, in the case of schizophrenia, it is also not advisable to use cannabis oil, despite some of its benefits for other conditions. And just to add — alcohol is also unfortunately bad for the condition, but not as bad as cannabis.

I found it important to emphasize that we tend to think of the opposite of drug addiction is abstinence. And that's where the biggest mistake is. In fact, the opposite of abstinence is connection. Therefore, it is of utmost importance that there be a change in habits; daily, activities, friendships, family, work, passions and so on. When you feel connected, part of a group (note that we all have that need to belong), when you feel loved and when you find meaning in life — the tendency to take drugs significantly reduces.

Many consume substances to avoid having to deal with the reality or the voids we have. So much so that they mention — when we're high, you don't need anyone and you can be good — it's the easiest way not to have to fight for a meaningful life — the easiest escape method. But unfortunately, being easier doesn't mean being beneficial.

Note that the behavioural theory — the one I follow — the most successful in behaviour change cases explains Operant conditioning and Classical Conditioning — I don't know if you've heard of it. From Pavlov, who experimented with dogs? He would ring a bell and then immediately put the food down for the dogs... after a while, regardless of whether he gave them food or not, the dogs salivated immediately when they heard the bell ring. This is to explain the association and immediate response of the brain. It would help to explore what kind of associations he makes that leads to his relapse in order to reverse it because it easily becomes automatic. For example, if the brain combines painting with Cannabis — when deciding to paint, the brain will touch the key that needs the substance.

The other factor that greatly influences behaviour change are rewards and punishments. From the moment there are unpleasant consequences for certain behaviours, the brain will try to avoid them because it will associate them with punishment.

If the person has plausible behaviour and is constantly rewarded, the brain will automatically encourage this behaviour simply because the brain loves compliments and gifts. That way, the incentive outweighs the punishments. That is, by focusing more on appraisals, we end up encouraging a certain behaviour and we are encouraging change. Instead of focusing on punishment and cutting off unwanted behaviour without encouraging other things.

I say this to suggest the following: When we talk to someone with an addiction, for example — if we are to say: "You should never smoke", we are actually commanding the brain to smoke. The brain interprets "Never Again" as "I want more than ever". So, this is not ideal. A better way of doing this would be — 1) Pulling him into his dreams, and as he sets his goals, he can easily see that in order to achieve them, he has to make certain adjustments in his life and one of them would be to stay sober. 2) Never frighten or demotivate them. That's why in AA they say — one day at a time, so we focus only on today, but again, the more we fight against something, the more it intensifies, so the focus and energy will no longer be used to cut what you don't want. But focus the energy on what you do want. And when designing goals, it's also important to divide them into phases, and each time he achieves a goal, even a minor one, he will have a reward. Having everything designed around increasing self-esteem will allow him to be more confident in himself, see his growth and feel a sense of fulfilment. The rewards have the same function.

When we have goals outlined, we know that we are winning vs when we have no goals and it becomes difficult to recognize the daily victories we are achieving.

# Dear Beautiful Soul

Thanks for your email of which you look for therapy for your loved one. Taking into consideration her age, I do recommend that whenever she feels ready — IF she does feel ready — she should contact me directly and we will schedule it.

Based on my experience, it is the most ideal method and a lot more efficient. If it is something she wants to do, she will contact me — if not, she won't. But if she ever does, she will then be a suitable client with a probability of a high success rate within a shorter period of time; on the other hand, if she comes because of reasons other than readiness and her own free will, together with the lack of commitment to tackle the situation, we will get nowhere and it can be a drag... neither of us want that. Therapy is a commitment, especially CBT as it involves homework between sessions which is a crucial requirement for great results.

I require that the client is CBT-ready, and when that becomes the situation at any point in their lives — you will be surprised by the efficiency and lifelong results. There is no rush into starting the process at all.

Remember: When the student is ready, the teacher appears.

I can understand the frustration you feel when you want to be there and help someone, and you want to try the solutions available, but if they are not ready, unfortunately we have to respect their time.

In the meantime, there is nothing more precious than knowledge regardless of whichever situation we are in — this includes depression. I do not perceive depression as a bad thing, I perceive it as necessary and valuable because it is there to tell us that something is not right or it might be time to evaluate things and change. Throughout the process that the person might not have the desire to be out and just wants to hibernate — it is also perfectly fine and ideal. When we are charged again, we get up and carry on with life. Again, the only secret lies in doing it wisely, seeking knowledge throughout, improving on the quality of our thoughts and... Hooray!

# Dear Beautiful Soul

We had a very interesting and constructive debate about relationships, and thought I would add some insights on it.

The perfect husband, perfect son-in-law and perfect lover — does not exist and if it ever appears to be that way, we need to worry — I repeat, it does not exist. And therefore, it shows that he is constantly playing a character — he is an actor. We are all actors to a very large extent but the average type of actor simply means adapting into each circumstance, meaning we behave differently in different scenarios, such as around a friend, lover, boss, employee, each member of the family and so forth — but without losing our essence nor lying about anything in the process — two very different scenarios and with significant differences. The case at hand does not appear to fall under that category — he appears to fully incarnate in each role which gives you the perception that he is living a double life.

Note, even though it may have felt that he was showing his essence more with you, it is not a clear indication that he really was. If he can act with others, he can act with you as well. In addition to that, if by any means his marital relationship does not work out and you happen to take over that role, it is clear what the role entails — lies — considering that we already have the job description for that position based on observation, endless evidence and facts.

I strongly believe that he shows significant Narcissistic and Sociopathic characteristics. These conditions are not a joke, they can do a lot of damage to the loved ones and, for many cases, people take too long to recover. I am not very fond of this because we cannot allow one crap experience to mess up our present and future or take away the happiness for future valuable experiences too. Time is limited for all of us, and it is precious. We will never get it back and I am also not very fond of continuing to allow people to have power over our happiness either, as the past hurt is more than enough. The analogy I can use for this is: You have a total of 1 million dollars in your bank account. Without your knowledge, someone has been hacking your account regularly by small daily amounts and 2 years later you find out that they have stolen 200 thousand. What would you do next? Give them the remaining 800 thousand or would you care for the remaining 800 thousand and make sure to not be scammed again? — Please try to contemplate on this and instead of money replace it with time. And this is what people constantly do — allow past experiences to mess up their current well-being and block any other positive experience that may come in the present or future.

Be aware that these personalities are not only selfish but their relationships are not usually based on the pure emotion only. Their self-interest and gains play a strong role in the choice of partners or relationships. It does not mean that they are monsters either — but they are Machiavellic — I am also not a fan of that trait because it goes hand in hand with lack of empathy — and may give the impression of being careless at certain stages, and it's true — they don't feel or mourn like the average person would.

These individuals are very clever and strategic. They understand clearly that in order to get what they get, they also needs to give, to motivate the others to give. But the nature of what they give doesn't weigh up. And as I mentioned in my article — it doesn't need to be necessarily money that feeds them, it can also be status, admiration — things that they value highly. 'The Sociopath World' is also part of my book and covered other aspects too — that is available on hardcopy and kindle version: "On the Road to Enlightenment: A Philosophical Way of Looking at Things".

There is no such thing as meeting our soulmate in the first weeks — perfect match, perfect everything, perfect love — that does not exist either. Based on my observations of people that have the tendency to stay with Narcs, I found that some do enjoy the Love Bombing a lot — because it gives someone adrenalin. When you are with a Con Artist they study you well, they hear about your interests, what you value, what your weaknesses are and they become exactly that — but they cannot keep that up for too long — so eventually the masks fall and you wake up.

The issue is that there is no cure for Sociopathy. Plus, if someone is a compulsive liar – in my view it is a serious condition as those are values that are a priority for me and I am not compromising that for anyone. And you know what? It is not our job to go around and try to fix our partners issues. These are changes that shall come from within. We cannot save anyone; each person needs to save themselves — as growth may happen but it cannot be forced. What we say in Penology (Criminology) is that the sentence must fit the crime. And for me, that is a serious crime.

I learnt that solid, healthy relationships take time to build. And it is important to understand — what exactly someone is looking for in a person? Being aware of it shall allow us to gain more control of who comes into our lives.

I found that it is important for someone to a) know what he or she wants, b) To not entertain or waste any time whatsoever with anyone that does not have the values that someone finds of high importance. Because, for as long as we spend time with an unsuitable match our doors are completely closed for the suitable match which is fully not ideal.

Finding a break up process difficult to endure, I do not believe that it is directly related to loving the partner. If I am to express the truth: Someone's brain, body, thoughts, emotions have been used to connecting things with the partner — like a drug. Many people acknowledge that certain drugs are not good for them and want to quit — but they express this assertively at that point until the body starts to crave. When this happens their desire to quit weakens and he has two choices:

1 - Go through the discomfort of craving the drug without doing anything about it and aware that if he goes through this period the body will also adapt and eventually it will go away.

2 - Relapse and avoid discomfort.

In other words — I think that the feelings of pain are directly related to a habit simply because habits are pretty challenging to break, but can be done successfully. So, this is all related to the meaning we give to whatever it is. Remember, symbols are given meaning by people. Without that, any symbol is meaningless.

I personally believe that you will enjoy the process — I love this, and CBT is awesome and life-changing, as once you master it, you shall be able to apply it continuously in all the different areas of your life.

Lastly, as a homework assignment:

1) Could you please take some time to contemplate on what are your strongest values are (these can be anything such as family, work, relationships, scuba diving... it can be anything)?

2) What do you look for in a partner?

3) What characteristics would you be willing to sacrifice in the name of love and what are the ones that you are not?

# CHAPTER 2

## On Relationships...

I just heard one of the most insightful speeches ever and had recently come to those conclusions too. When we meet someone and start becoming infatuated, we automatically become blind and irrational, therefore, it becomes a bit difficult to judge their behaviour at that very stage. Many people have the tendency to keep it to themselves and not share about the new relationship with their loved ones which later leads them into trouble. On a different note, they may introduce the crush to loved ones during the infatuation state and when the loved ones spot red flags, they tend to ignore it or defend him by saying things such as: he is different when they are alone.

From the moment we move away from our loved ones when we meet someone, get warned by loved ones, isolate ourselves and constantly find excuses — that shall be the number one Red Flag! Interesting enough is the fact that: 1) We become irrational and unable to make rational decisions or evaluations; 2) Under the effect, we do turn against the loved ones and somehow tend to believe that our loved ones do not want our happiness —That is the most ridiculous form of thinking; 3) A large majority of the times — our loved ones were correct and we feel silly at a later stage. So yes, instead of trying to prove something, being in full defensive mode, why not pay attention and try to understand where our loved ones are coming from?

I found that the secret lies in introducing the person to our loved ones beforehand, before getting into the infatuation mode so we can assess it while rational as from the moment someone gets into the "love spell" the capacity to make judgements diminishes greatly. If by any means we feel reluctant to introduce the person to the loved ones – it is not a good sign and this needs to be evaluated.

# CHAPTER 3

# My Public Speaking phobia...

I once decided to send a video to my cousin — and had chosen the method to make the message more personal and valuable. When they saw the video and thanked me — they also mentioned that I do sound and look very good at a camera and asked — why not start making more videos for my career as a psychologist? As they said that, it activated the desire of doing so — and as a result I got up, touched on my makeup found the best angle at home and made a video about Cognitive Behavioural Therapy, I posted on YouTube and sent to my friends too. I got a lot of warmth from people and compliments regarding my confidence doing the video and how it takes courage to do so, so one of my replies with regards to that was:

Thank you, well it was not overnight and I had always wanted to start doing it — and probably took years till I felt this ready — as it took personal development, growth and daily knowledge.

And that was my first time trying it on and I post it — also to stretch myself too and move away from my comfort zone.

I always had a public speaking phobia — which is another work I had to do to myself.

Better to do it with fear than not doing it and one day in our deathbed ask ourselves: what if I had done it?

I call my fear of public speaking a phobia because the intensity of my anxiety to simply ask a question to a teacher, express an opinion or an idea a couple of years back— was at the highest... My heart would beat SO much, my voice would shake, my body — it was ridiculous. And you will be surprised that the majority of people have the same fear too! It is the most common fear/anxiety and some hide better than others — including public speakers. But — it becomes tricky when that fear interferes with your dreams and goals. And in my case — it was holding me back and stopping me from achieving my dream. When I started becoming a psychologist, can you imagine the anxiety I had with my first clients? Successful people, full of experience and all — so it went down to my low self-esteem and what I was telling myself. I had to change my thought process and improve the quality of my thoughts.

Asking myself things such as: "What am I anxious about? I spent my whole life learning this stuff, I know this stuff through and I am the expert in this. If they approached me, it is because they feel that I will bring value into their lives, and the truth is, the teachings are very powerful. Do not pressure yourself and expect yourself to be loved by all as that is irrational — it is very difficult, if not impossible, to be able to be liked by all. Do not pressure yourself to be perfect because it is irrational too — there are no perfect beings. Focus on what you are doing, give your best and that is all. I would prefer to be 'loved', but if that does not happen — it is really not the end of the world."

SO, I would change all my negative thinking and preach those words to myself, constantly — and naturally, it went away and I don't remember the last time I felt anxious at work. I managed to eliminate it pretty quickly.

Also, through exposure and repeatedly doing it.

So, public speaking follows the same route — I forced myself to be in those situations and it had reduced significantly — but the work is not done. There is still some work but I am positive that I will get there through training my brain to be kind with myself.

Yes, and understand that it is really not realistic that everyone will find us interesting. People are different, and they connect with different things. And that is actually extremely positive because it leaves room for everyone to be able to express and do what they love because there is always a group of people that will enjoy it — which is what matters.

And others not enjoying it is perfectly fine. But the problem may lie in how we interpret some people not enjoying it.

For example, irrational Thinking: Some people did not like me and found me boring, therefore, I am not good enough and I am boring. Rational Thinking: Some people did not like me and found me boring and it is not pleasant but it is expected because not everyone has the same interests and can relate to my stuff. That is okay and it does not define me in any way.

You will always find haters and will do everything to bring you down. So, the secret is also to be selective on the criticisms.

It's easy to criticise while sitting behind a PC.

I would challenge them to get off the chair and do a better job. Then we can talk.

EVERYONE HAS A CALLING.

What happens is that they sabotage themselves and let others sabotage them too. Because people will always put you down, tell you that your plans will not work, find obstacles and so forth. We need to fully believe in ourselves — because we do have a calling.

I have a client that was once crying and telling me that he always drops his studies and he can't achieve anything — big procrastinator in that area. I told him that — it seems that he is not interested in what he is studying — that's why he doesn't pay attention — and that is natural to be demotivated into what you don't love.

He continued to blame himself and saying that I don't get it, but the problem is with him. Eventually, I asked him — what he loves doing, doesn't miss and goes through with it?

He says: Sports!

So, if he is so terrible at paying attention, and not good enough at all, how come that does not happen for sports? — Lightbulb moment — Work in what you love and finish the story. Make a career out of it and done.

He had never thought about that at all but that opened his horizons. So, this is to say that — we simply sabotage ourselves by not making the rational evaluation of what is happening and the reasons for our behaviours. People that have been diagnosed with Attention deficit hyperactivity disorder (ADHD) as an example, make great salespeople and TV presenters. Why adjust your nature — for what? Those invented disorders are ways to make money. I am in the field and I promise this to you. It's a business. The pharmaceutical industry is the most profitable organization and if they ally with psychiatrists everyone gets rich! So pay attention and be careful to not take things on face value.

# CHAPTER 4

## Are we defined by the past?

Psychoanalysis differs from Cognitive Behavioural Therapy as it places a lot of focus on the early experiences and spends too much time there — meaning the therapy process can easily take many months. I do spend some time there but I don't think that it's overall necessary to spend too much time digging the past unless it is an important requirement to solve the problem. Note that stating that the past is not important, is a clear fallacy but it is important to understand that it is not fully responsible for the outcome of things.

The idea is to try to remove ourselves from the victimhood mindset and blaming people or events for the current situation — but rather take charge of it. I shall repeat —

even though those things have had a great influence on the current situation — they are not fully responsible for the current situation.

Based on some interviews and live therapies with Albert Ellis on Rational Emotive Behavioural Therapy, Marsha Linehan on Dialectical Behavioural Therapy, and many others, I don't see any of them placing focus on childhood. I see them speaking in a very present-oriented manner, and placing great focus on the core beliefs. In one of the therapy sessions when Ellis asked the client for an example, he clearly stated: "Not an ancient one...".

Surely there are other forms of therapy that place greater focus on earlier or childhood experiences, although, in my current approach to things, I do not recall in any of my treatment plans to spend time in early childhood. Of course, it may happen – naturally, if we find the need to, but I do it mostly with the purpose of making connections and usually bring the client back to the present moment. When the client feels the need to explore their childhood, you may find some CBT therapists that choose to refer them to other therapists that place higher focus on early experiences, and when the clients are what we call "CBT ready", ready for change, they can go back.

In my opinion, it's very tricky because even though we might think that the recollection of events is accurate, based on a number of studies — our memory is not trustworthy, plus the client is sharing a perspective too or how they felt. And I always try to explain to them how the memory works and how inaccurate it is so they are aware. Many studies have proven that with time, our recollection of events becomes more and more distorted.

I was speaking to a woman who developed a strong dislike for males and she told me that it is because she was molested as a toddler. And I asked her about the experience and she told me that she did not know but she found out through hypnotherapy — Regression. I got so upset because this hypnotherapist has created this idea in her mind about something that the brain could have made up — because the memory is not reliable. So, they basically created a problem — she wants nothing to do with relationships now. I also believe that the "Why" question is unprofitable as it leads to too much victimhood and excuses. Whether through Hypnosis or Talk therapy — those experiences are no longer accurate, unfortunately. But note, I don't dismiss it but I try to explain to them how the process works, so they are also able to let go if by any chance they believe it's fully responsible. The majority of my clients love my approach because many don't enjoy that nor do they want that childhood dwelling — they want something practical — and many come to me because of that specifically. But, of course, we can't make everybody happy — that's why we are all different, so it gives room for everyone to succeed.

It is extremely important to find out what school of thought someone follows — as you can easily get caught up with a method that it is not your preferred method. When referring to Psychoanalytic Approaches — I would be biased when giving my opinion as I follow CBT, which is evidence-based and it is the exact opposite of Psychoanalysis. Although I do not think that Freud's contribution should be ignored nor dismissed because he definitely is one of the biggest contributors to the field of Psychology — and for some people, that method is ideal.

Regression can lead to false memories and Re-traumatization. The outcome that I hear often is "blaming" — parents, childhood experiences, past-life experiences (continuous blaming to justify the behaviour) — and absolutely nothing resolved. So, they move from sitting with a problem, to a much bigger problem as the responsibility is then assigned to things that are not applicable in the here and now. I find this terrible, as it does the opposite of empowering and removes responsibility from oneself to transform ourselves. So, what was the point exactly?

In my mind, the idea is to solve the problem. When I do have debates with people that follow that school of thought, they believe that they are better off as they keep the client for over a year easily as the treatment takes forever. I totally disagree with this approach to counselling. I do not see how this group could be happy with that, nor see it as an advantage as it does not show efficiency but dragging of the problem. Don't they want results? I can't imagine myself as a client sitting every week for a year and speaking about "when I was a child..." and never mind the fact that I don't remember much at all! I don't even remember what I had for dinner 3 days ago, how on earth will I remember what happened decades ago? So much so that it is common to see people that experienced the same event describe the experience differently.

You can recognize straight away in their speech if they follow those approaches. Things such as: "Person X, is behaving like that towards me and I am positive that it has to do with her relationship with her father when she was a child".— When I hear stuff like that I become speechless — how do you know that that is the cause, to speak with such conviction? — Plus, for every single disorder or condition, it is usually a combination of factors — and all of it is just guessing anyways! Again, that is why, we as Life Coaches normally find the "why" question very unproductive — as it always leads to excuses and blaming. "What is happening", "How" — makes a lot more sense.

My role as a therapist is usually to be extremely empathetic about the circumstances, understand how the past events may have influenced the circumstances, tell them to stop beating themselves up about it, be kind with themselves and understand that thankfully those experiences happened in the past and as much as it may appear that it determines the present it does not, they have a choice and I want to give the power back to them

Ellis developed the ABC Model. The ABC Model is where — A stands for Antecedent (i.e. the situation that triggers the response) B stands for Beliefs (our thoughts/interpretation of the situation/event) C stands for Consequences (the way we feel or behave).

And when they move from the A – C to the B – C connection — the results are awesome. I never said that we neglect, don't care but the truth is it is not always necessary explore early experiences in depth to solve the problem. I also use Neuro-linguistic programming (NLP) and there are clients that we managed to solve a whole bunch of issues without me knowing much about their lives through the tools — whether NLP or CBT. if we think about it — even with hypnosis many times we can still cure the stuff without knowing too much about it — as the client does the work themselves and we guide them. Albert Ellis perceives the therapist as a teacher. As once we master the tools and how they work with one example — we can then practice with a whole bunch of them — ourselves.

On a recent conversation with a client on how childhood trauma may sometimes be the perfect excuse for psychopaths to carry out atrocities, she had shared that in South Africa she had a teacher who shared that he comes from a very traditional and pure racist Afrikaans family and upbringing and therefore he used to have a very negative and strong connotation towards people of colour. When the students asked him how come he is in a multi-racial environment his reply was:

"There comes a point in our lives that we can no longer blame our parents for our choices, perceptions and behaviours. From a certain stage you are able to think for yourself. And being at University and engaging with people with colour I found that the idea that they sold to me was a hoax. We are all too similar in many ways as after all we are all part of the human race."

This man understands the concept of victimhood, accountability and responsibility. And if he was able to use his own judgement and shape his ideas on his own regardless of the conservative upbringing he had, this is pure evidence that all of us have the exact same capability to do so.

Viktor Frankl is an Austrian neurologist and psychiatrist as well as a Holocaust survivor. He is an Existential psychologist and founder of Logotherapy; a form of psychotherapy that he developed after surviving Nazi concentration camps in the 1940s. "Logos" is the Greek word for meaning and Logotherapy involves helping the clients to find personal meaning in life.

"The experiences of camp life show that man does have a choice of action. There were enough examples, often of a heroic nature, which proved that apathy could be overcome, irritability suppressed. Man can preserve a vestige of spiritual freedom, of independence of mind, even in such terrible conditions of psychic and physical stress. We who lived in concentration camps can remember the men who walked through the huts comforting others, giving away their last piece of bread. They may have been few in numbers, but they offer sufficient proof that everything can be taken from a man but one thing: the last of the human freedoms — to choose one's attitude in any given set of circumstances, to choose one's own way... It is this spiritual freedom — which cannot be taken away — that makes life meaningful and purposeful."

— Viktor Frankl, Man's Search for Meaning

Frankl believed that when we can no longer change a situation, we are forced to change ourselves.

Based on Logotherapy, that meaning can be discovered in three distinct ways:

1.  By creating a work or doing a deed.

2.  By experiencing something or encountering someone.

3.  By the attitude that we take toward unavoidable suffering.

# CHAPTER 5

# Is it too late to follow our passion?

It is the most common thing amongst mental health practitioners to always feel that they need to add more to their knowledge to be ready — and somehow, it becomes never-ending. I also had the same tendency as plenty of the people I studied with.

If I have to think about over 100 people I did the training with in London and South Africa – only about 10 people likely pursued Sema career. At University, there were hundreds of us, but hardly anyone followed the path. No one seemed to have the patience to persist and preferred to take the easy way out by choosing another field. People continuously procrastinate, and through that very process, you forget the knowledge and lose the drive.

Each of us have a great deal of experience behind us — although different from one another, and that is what makes us special.

What will make you special and successful? This background of knowledge and experiences that you have been accumulating over the years.

Don't allow your brain to lie to you and fill you with limiting beliefs because all your brain is sensing is danger and threat — as you are suggesting getting out of your comfort zone. So, it is your duty to ensure your brain that it is not dangerous and it will be fine. From the moment you take steps, your brain will get used to it and the new set of behaviours move to your comfort zone too.

For many years I have been suffering as I chose to use the iPhone with all its limitations and battery life of a quarter of the day — which automatically makes it unreliable!!! I thought it was normal until I moved to Samsung — with a battery life of over 24 hours and almost 48 hours!!!

Never mind the amount of information I keep on losing because of the famous iCloud and lost everything one more time!!! Customer Service — even they have limitations!!

Luckily it happened enough to make me used to it.

The amount of restrictions and inflexibility!! Chargers that last a month!!! The camera quality!!

This is just to show the power of marketing, capable of fully manipulating us and give us the illusion that it's the best — even though evidence shows otherwise.

It is indeed interesting how our brain works, that enjoys comfort zone and what is familiar with, as a result it tends to show resistance for change even when it is clear that it is the best solution. And this happens in all areas of our lives, every single time we are supposed to step outside our comfort zone, the brain perceives it as a threat and finds excuses to remain where we are. And therefore, it is our duty to keep our brain aware that there is no "danger" and it will be fine.

This is an example of being the Master of your mind as opposed to a slave of our thoughts and feelings. Soon enough, once we move out of it and practice it, those same things move to our comfort zone too.

So, for as long as we accept discomfort and not perceive it as the end of the world, it soon turns it into comfort.

# CHAPTER 6

# Be Kind to Yourself

Oh, wow. I find that you tend to not look at yourself from a rational point of view and you really fail to see that you are GOLD. Yes, you have been going through a tough time, yes, you may have lashed out on people that you love, yes, you may have sounded negative at times, but this is because you are human. And it's a phase you are going through such as the hatching point when the caterpillar is becoming a butterfly. It's difficult, is it not? Although necessary. And once you start recognizing who you really are, you will want to be next to someone that grows with you and that you can count on. Not someone that only wants the "good" as this is not realistic for any relationship. I am seriously struggling to understand why you fail to see what we see when we look at you? I am not understanding why you are selling a Ferrari for the price of a Toyota! Why? You are telling yourself these things, setting your price tag, carrying it with you and probably influencing others to perceive you the way you feel.

Think of someone you love dearly. What if she is in your situation and she tells you that she is not "good enough". How would you respond to that?

How do you respond to yourself? What's the difference?

One thing I learnt – being a narcissist is not all that bad! We can learn from the narcs too in how they put themselves first before anything and make sure that they get the best in everything. When I was in Lisbon, I decided to focus on Harvey Specter from Suits – observe how he carries himself, how he loves himself, the image he sends to people and to become as confident as he is — of course, by ignoring what I do not want to assimilate. And really taking accountability for behaviours I may have had in the past that were not plausible.

Please forgive yourself for making such terrible assumptions about yourself, for bringing yourself down at times, for being unkind to yourself and rigid to your special self. Please promise to be kind and loving to yourself.

You are fallible human being worthy of unconditional love.

# CHAPTER 7

# The Message or the Messenger?

The first idea I shared in my previous book "On the Road to Enlightenment" is in relation to the importance of focusing on the message and not the messenger, as a large majority of people have the tendency to adore and focus on the messenger instead.

And what does this lead to? Idealization and unrealistic expectations towards the qualities of another human being. The belief that the messenger must hold certain characteristics that takes them closer to perfection.

As a result there is pressure from society for the messenger to be a certain way, higher probability of criticisms when people realize that they are mere human-beings and expectations from people based on what they believe the characteristics of the messenger should be.

On my book launch in Johannesburg, one of the participants asked me what surprised me the most when I went to the monastery in Nepal. My reply was: I was expecting to find perfect people. That the monks would be enlightened people enjoying the perfect bliss. But, I found mere human-beings like all of us, with their great qualities and imperfections too, humble but with tempers too. And only years later, I understood that, that is enlightenment. To accept our nature as fallible human beings worthy of unconditional love and compassion. To stop fighting our nature as human beings and simply – BE. Stop trying to change others so they have a checklist and only once all the items on the list are ticked shall someone be worthy of unconditional love.

I still recall the monks and nuns sharing their stories that they find super hilarious of being out somewhere and strangers coming up to them and opening up about all their problems expecting them to guide them. And they get so surprised and wonder: What makes them think that I can solve their issues? Or that I have all the answers?

One of the most important things for me is to never lose my authenticity and never portray myself as something that I am not. I aim to show my human side with my strengths and weaknesses just like all of us on planet earth. And I am worthy of unconditional love regardless of how screwed up

I am as a human being, it is my nature after all and there is no escape.

In fact, my understanding of Enlightenment is simply to be awake. Being awake is to be aware, to be realistic, to understand the world and nature for what it is and most importantly understand our human nature.

Being able to detach from the Ego comes naturally as a consequence. We do not chase detachment, we do not chase a balanced mind, we do not chase healthy relationships, we do not fight against depression or anxiety, and all these things are achieved as consequence. The same way that if you water a tree daily, bearing fruits shall be the consequence of it.

# CHAPTER 8

## Maktub

There is one very important aspect that has been making a huge difference in my achievements: as soon as I have an idea that is matured and I can visualize it correctly, I move directly to execution — even if it means setting deadlines and commit to them as I plan. But I decided to eliminate procrastination from my life.

Putting the teachings into practice is a must if we ever want to see great results.

All the strengths and talents we have can be used as expert knowledge and seriously help others. Well, helping as a friend and giving advice is different to when we do it as a coach or therapist.

As for myself, when I got back from London it became a great struggle to continue to be an employee, so I quit. I essentially became a starving artist. I took advantage of being unemployed in order to write my first book and I managed to do so. Thanks to all the closed doors that I had — even as a psychologist, I tried everywhere and begged for internships — just something – But I got nothing! You have absolutely no idea how many doors were closed for me over the years.

So, I was forced to follow my path. In other words, the inflation forced me to become an entrepreneur — I did not have much of a choice.

**Maktub**, it was written.

Surprisingly, I found that opportunities are infinite. We just need to grab them, know what we want and pursue in that direction. By taking one step every day eventually we shall arrive regardless of how long it takes.

Thanks to all the doors that were closed for me over the years I was finally able to have time and pursue my dream of becoming a writer and write my first book. Thanks to all the "Nos" that I got throughout these years, I was able to become an entrepreneur, open my own practice and provide a variety of services based on my strengths. And when you do something from your heart, excellence is inevitable as you go the extra mile willingly; you find meaning in life.

I cannot be more grateful for all the things that did not work out in my life as that was extremely essential for my understanding of things, for the path I decided to take and most importantly to develop strong unconditional self-love. And therefore, I have learnt to not rate a situation as good or bad as I do not have enough knowledge. Wanting something does not mean that it is the best thing to have. We do not know. And as I look back into the recollection of memories and events, it can all be summarized by: **Maktub.**

# CHAPTER 9

# The Mask

---

1. What is more important for you in a person?

2. What catches your attention when you observe someone?

3. Superficial beauty or anything beyond that?

I enjoy playing with people's perceptions and see how easy it is for others to perceive me the way that I choose to be perceived. It is so easy, people create a judgement on each other based on how well you carry yourself, your dress code, your hair, how you speak and what you say even if the interaction is simply for 5 min. This is the act that we all put on depending on the circumstances. The secret is to be fully aware that it's an act and the reality is that we all do that, whether consciously or unconsciously.

Have you noticed that a job position is referred to as — role? Which means, during working hours the role that you will play will be as an administration officer and at home you are simply Mr. John.

On the movie V for Vendetta, the character V and Evey spent a considerable amount of time together within a year, they both played very strong and great roles in each other's lives and they fell in love with each other. Although, throughout the entire time, V wore a mask and therefore, Evey had never seen his face. On the day of the revolution, their last day together, Evey surprised him in his home and played on of their favourite songs called Bird gherl. V suggested that he had heard all of the songs in his collection but had never danced to any of them, and invited her to dance with him. As they danced Evey attempted to remove his mask. V stopped her and said:

Vendetta: "There is a face beneath this mask, but it isn't me. I'm no more that face than I am the muscles beneath it, or the bones beneath that."

This is one of my favourite passages from the movie V for Vendetta that caught my full attention.

What do I truly love about V?

— Throughout the entire movie, V did not uncover any part of his body, except his hands that were burnt as he was once at a fire. This means that my opinion of him is fully based on his mannerisms, behaviours, characteristics, intelligence, eloquence, passions and so forth, and yet, he is my favourite character in the history of movies, which I do not get tired of watching over and over again.

Man is least himself when he talks in his own person. Give him a mask, and he will tell you the truth. — Oscar Wilde

# Conclusion

This book is inspired by real cases, but has been manipulated to protect and maintain confidentiality. It has been written as a self-help guide for you in order to allow you to gain a wise insight into many areas of your life.

I believe that the educational system should have been able to teach everyone about emotional intelligence and knowledge of the brain to allow most people to live a happier life and reduce all the unnecessary suffering most of us go through.

The purpose of this book is to help you gain as much benefit as you can through the countless communications on various topics, conditions and struggles that will allow you to apply the teachings in different areas of your life and therefore, bring great value into your life.

Remember to please be kind to yourself. The same way that you are kind to your loved ones and always elevate them, share kind and truthful words with them, and always try to make them aware of their value and uniqueness – I challenge you to use that very same quality and energy on being kind to your own self.

This book is dedicated to you: The reader.

# Acknowledgements

I would like to give a special thanks to my lovely parents, Selma Ismael Sema and Roodolf Raston for being a rock in my life, for being extremely precious to me and for the infinite support at all times.

I would like to thank all my clients for being amazing, for the loyalty, for the endless support, trust and constant recommendations as they have been highly responsible for my rapid growth.

To my Family and Friends, thank you for all the support and encouragement throughout my journey.

Love and Light

Sharlene Sema Raston

www.ingramcontent.com/pod-product-compliance
Lightning Source LLC
Chambersburg PA
CBHW031233250726
48655CB00005B/1930